Praise for

Consciousness Rising

'If you suddenly feel crazy, weird, ungrounded, sense far more than meets the eye, and can't help but question everything you were taught to believe and consider important, you are not losing your mind. You are waking up. Don't panic. Nicky Sutton's wonderful, life-saving book, Consciousness Rising, is the best, most practical, grounded guide you will find to navigate the disruptive, liberating, and soul-empowering journey that is underway.'

SONIA CHOQUETTE, BESTSELLING AUTHOR OF *ASK YOUR GUIDES*

'An ESSENTIAL read for anyone on the spiritual awakening path. This brilliant and unique guide walks you – step by step – through the most important transformation of your life.'

VICTOR ODDO, COACH AND SOCIAL MEDIA INFLUENCER

Consciousness Rising

Consciousness Rising

Guiding You through Spiritual Awakening and beyond

NICKY SUTTON

HAY HOUSE

Carlsbad, California • New York City
London • Sydney • New Delhi

Published in the United Kingdom by:
Hay House UK Ltd, The Sixth Floor, Watson House,
54 Baker Street, London W1U 7BU
Tel: +44 (0)20 3927 7290; Fax: +44 (0)20 3927 7291; www.hayhouse.co.uk

Published in the United States of America by:
Hay House Inc., PO Box 5100, Carlsbad, CA 92018-5100
Tel: (1) 760 431 7695 or (800) 654 5126
Fax: (1) 760 431 6948 or (800) 650 5115; www.hayhouse.com

Published in Australia by:
Hay House Australia Pty Ltd, 18/36 Ralph St, Alexandria NSW 2015
Tel: (61) 2 9669 4299; Fax: (61) 2 9669 4144; www.hayhouse.com.au

Published in India by:
Hay House Publishers India, Muskaan Complex,
Plot No.3, B-2, Vasant Kunj, New Delhi 110 070
Tel: (91) 11 4176 1620; Fax: (91) 11 4176 1630; www.hayhouse.co.in

Text © Nicky Sutton, 2021

A catalogue record for this book is available from the British Library.

Tradepaper ISBN: 978-1-78817-478-7
E-book ISBN: 978-1-78817-482-4
Audiobook ISBN: 978-1-78817-599-9

Interior illustrations: Shutterstock.com

Printed and bound by CPI Group (UK) Ltd, Croydon, CR0 4YY

To my dear husband, Antti, thank you for everything.

Contents

List of Exercises and Practices

Introduction

The process of spiritual awakening is like the metamorphosis of a butterfly. Just like the former caterpillar, you're undergoing a profound transformation and becoming a different kind of being. Once you discover your true colors, you'll be ready to take flight and embody your limitless purpose and potential.

Have you been through spiritual awakening? Are you going through it now? If your sense of self is dissolving or your perceptions of reality and purpose are transforming uncontrollably, then it's possible. Whether your awakening is challenging, blissful, or somewhere in between, this book is here to support you through awakening and beyond. My core message to you is, you're not alone, you're not crazy, and you can achieve joy and fulfillment.

I describe spiritual awakening as a shift in consciousness, where your beliefs and perceptions move from an atheist, materialist, or religious point of view, to a more spiritual, holistic, metaphysical, and esoteric one. 'You have an irresistible urge to discover a more authentic, loving, and extraordinary version of yourself and reality. This metamorphosis can blow your life and sense of self to pieces or gently enhance your perceptions. Either way, you're changing, and there's no going back.

Everyone's spiritual awakening is different, and it's not easy to cover everybody's unique experiences, reactions, and path into awakening. Nevertheless, no matter how your awakening unfolds, this book will provide you with knowledge, inspiration, and guidance, as well as various examples of other people's experiences to inspire you.

I wish I'd had a helping hand during my awakening, especially during the more challenging stages. Hence, I write this for you. I don't claim to be a guru or a master, or to have attained enlightenment. I'm just someone who has experienced a mind-shattering transformation and feels compelled to guide and assist others undergoing the same process. Since my awakening, I've accumulated quite an online audience, proving to me, at least, the need for this material. I have conducted hundreds of one-on-one sessions in spiritual guidance, past-life regression, and hypnosis healing, which have added to my understanding of awakening as experienced by many individuals.

Seemingly, an increasing number of people are encountering this phenomenon. As our thoughts, feelings, and intentions sweep through our collective consciousness, many more awakenings are being triggered. As our world drowns in consumerism and seemingly endless political, economic, and social turmoil, we watch the leaders of humanity bicker and squabble like actors in a crummy TV show. But perhaps a new way of life is dawning – a renewed perception of the world – as we discover ancient spiritual wisdom, holistic well-being, and a more heart-led existence.

Spiritual awakening is one of the most meaningful and transformative experiences a person can have. We awaken to valuable knowledge (such as the immortality of the soul), psychic phenomena, the law of attraction, the energetic nature of reality, synchronicities, inner healing, the extent of societal corruption, past lives, and much more. We move through every extreme of emotion, from hopeless despair to divine bliss, as everything seems to fall apart, and we reconstruct ourselves anew. 'Who am I?' we ask. That's a good question. New ways of perceiving ourselves and life also dawn on us as we learn to explore our infinite true selves, transcend illusions, and release resistance.

We each find our own truths, so don't take my words as 'gospel,' but, like me, continue learning, experiencing, and practicing your own spirituality on your adventure toward wholeness and self-actualization. The initial acutely transformative stages do pass and reveal that awakening is a never-ending process. To reiterate, once initiated, our awakening to new ideas and possibilities continues – always. Life is a voyage of learning and experience, but it's our approach to it that makes all the difference.

As a child, I felt like something was 'off'– that there was a hidden truth behind the concept of reality that was being sold to me. Something that I couldn't see, touch, or learn about at school. At the age of nine, I was fascinated when my mother asked an earthbound spirit, George, to leave our new home;

he was upsetting my sister and me. Mum was neither spiritual nor religious but did occasionally sense spirits. A drawer had slammed shut on its own in my room, and objects would disappear, then reappear in unusual places. My older sister had similar experiences with George. While she tried to sleep, the lid of a ceramic pot would turn around on its base, making a squeaking, grinding noise. We were both fed up and frightened. George, the previous owner of the property, had passed away just weeks before we moved in, so Mum stood in the hall and read out George's widow's new address, assuming that he couldn't find her. By the next day, the ghostly phenomena had stopped, and Mum was very pleased with herself. Pam, George's widow, came to a Christmas party at our house some months later, and Mum apprehensively told her what had happened. Pam replied, 'Yes, he arrived with me soon after, thank you!'

This and other early experiences piqued my interest in the paranormal and metaphysical, and I was sure there were further profound aspects to life awaiting discovery. At age 11, I purchased my first set of tarot cards, and at age 15, a book by psychic medium John Edward. Mediumship isn't everyone's cup of tea, but for me, learning of his experiences and abilities was a tremendous relief. I realized I wasn't crazy, having felt different from other kids in many ways, and a little peacefulness entered my life. But still, I had no full-blown awakening; it took a traumatic event to initiate that.

Fast-forward to my late twenties. I had two kids and a relatively happy home with my partner. Then, our relationship broke down after a period of turmoil, my father died, and, for various reasons, I had to move halfway up the country. The sheer shock of all this and the hardships that followed caused my inner world to collapse. As if on autopilot, I was taking care of my children as best I could, but I felt lost, numb, and misunderstood. Synchronistically, I discovered spiritual material, channelings, and books that stripped away my perception of life and who or what I thought I was. It was a double whammy, a traumatic event leading to my drastic transformation. My spiritual awakening had begun. Now, years later, life is fulfilling and rewarding while still being a work in progress. Full of vital energy, I can be of service to others while taking great care of myself and my family.

Your awakening path will likely show you shadowy aspects of your subconscious mind on the way to emotional wholeness and self-realization. This was what it was like for me. You can move through awakening into fulfillment and abundance with powerful realizations and practices, such as the ones I describe in this book.

Spiritual awakening can be overwhelming and, at times, seemingly unforgiving, but trust in yourself and the process, and be proud that you're daring to face and transcend your illusions. It's happening for a good reason – you're stepping into your true self and infinite possibilities.

~

Chapter 1

The Awakening

Awakening could be the next stage in humanity's evolution. If the nature of life and consciousness are indeed spiritual, then far too many of us are sleeping through it. We are likely limiting our abilities and potential by allowing our genuine essence to go unacknowledged.

Our way of life could be significantly different if we based our aims and activities around a spiritual reality rather than a material one. We would nurture psychic and intuitive senses from birth (our innate abilities), encourage cooperation more than competition, prioritize emotional support and inclusion, and respect and live in harmony with nature, to name just a few adjustments. Global society is extremely left-brained in structure, based on physical assumptions and acquisitions, and prizes masculine energy above the feminine. I'm not referring to men over women in this particular instance, rather the universal energies we use to create. Masculine energies being drive, will, and determination; and feminine being creative, emotional, and intuitive.

During spiritual awakening, we reevaluate old beliefs and discover new ones that intuitively *feel* right. We also remember wisdom buried deep within. The funny thing is that, once awakening happens, most people come to very similar conclusions and foster highly comparable understandings. Instead of assimilating a particular set of beliefs, though, we explore our own. Our new perspectives are usually backed up by personal experience, perhaps mystical or paranormal in nature; 'proof' provided by others that holds truth; or by theoretical science that attempts to explain the metaphysical.

Here, I put forward the case that modern spirituality is not religion. Hear me out – I'm not refuting any religions here. Spirituality seems to lack characteristics associated with religion. It has no:

- rigid framework of belief

- requirement for faith in any doctrine

- compulsory sacred texts, teachings, gods, ancient masters, rituals, or ceremonies (you can choose your preference)

- worshipping

- submission to authority

- judgment from a higher power

People simply needed a name for it, and that ended up being 'spirituality,' which, owing to its extensive spectrum of preferences and practices, is more like 'self-development' than a religion. Spirituality brings people together who have come to similar, but not necessarily the same, conclusions. Many people resonate with aspects of various religions and integrate their favorites into their spiritual practice. I love many aspects of Hinduism and Buddhism. Spirituality is figuring out your own personal truth and living by it.

The intensity of the initial stages of awakening varies significantly depending on a person's background and personality. Some take awakening in stride, don't surprise easily, and don't find it emotionally draining; others are so taken aback that it throws them into a period of turmoil. And many people's experiences lie between these two poles.

My awakening was on the level of a bombshell revolution of the mind. Although I'd had a sneaky suspicion all my life about the spiritual nature of reality, had seen several apparitions, and experienced accurate mediumship readings, it was still, strangely enough, a complete surprise! I thought 'spirit' or spiritualism was the extent of hidden knowledge, but that was just the tip of the iceberg. I had always doubted my intuitive knowing of the metaphysical nature of reality since others around me had little interest in it. This made me think I might be imagining it. Having felt like a 'weirdo' forever, I was immeasurably grateful that awakening showed me that I was perhaps remembering spiritual wisdom forgotten at birth.

Awakening can happen to anyone, regardless of age, race, gender, background, or birthplace. I have interacted with many young people, often clients or those following my online content, who are traversing the awakening process. It's wonderful to observe how intuitively wise they are. The quick-fix lifestyle that companies promote doesn't fool them, and they are searching for greater meaning. Social media's 'get likes for self-worth' sales pitch has many people, young and older, suspecting that happiness is probably not found there, and they yearn for something more consciously and intellectually stimulating. No matter the age of our bodies, we can still be old souls. Wise and loving souls walk among us every day, seeking to positively influence the direction of humanity.

There are still many unanswered questions in the universe. For those who wonder about the meaning of life, our purpose, the existence of God, fate, and destiny, spirituality can offer answers. For many of us, the not knowing is too much to handle, so upon awakening, we dive right in.

What Is Spiritual Awakening?

Because kids are very impressionable, when they are born into society they naturally adopt its particular belief systems. Likewise, on the family level, even if your parents hold attitudes, values, and beliefs that differ from the general population, you'll still absorb them like a sponge, trying your best to do what people expect of you. The 'little you' didn't know any different and was trying to make sense of, and fit into, a confusing world.

Sit for a moment and try to identify some of the programming you unwittingly received. Sure, some of it was very positive. For example, you mustn't pull the dog's tail, eat off the floor, or run across the road. You should be kind to people and remember to say please and thank you. These are everyday things. As you grew older, you might also have accepted being unquestioning of authority or established science, that anything beyond the physical and measurable is merely woo-woo, and that success and material goods equal happiness. These are commonly adopted beliefs.

Well-meaning people gave you a framework of perceptions as they helped induct you into life on Earth. These perceptions formed a stable foundation upon which to move forward as you began to make your way in the world. However, it only takes one triggering event to initiate a shift in a few of these perceptions, and the rest cascade around you.

Spiritual awakening is an initiation into a new dimension of awareness as a free-thinking, sovereign individual, who is also one with the whole. It's finding your individuality while casting off the group or societal mentality. The demanding nature of the initial stages of awakening echoes the hardships and challenges of an initiation. Once through it, you're free to assume your distinctiveness and fortitude, in service to others and service to self. Paradoxically, individuation often leads us toward unity and oneness as we find our place and purpose within the all.

You may have noticed to a greater or lesser degree that deep unhappiness is endemic within society, and that something has to give. Perhaps this shows that we are not all living our truth, because, in my experience, those who awaken to spiritual exploration and practice find more happiness day to day, or at least are on the path toward it.

Awakening Is Beyond Words, but in a Nutshell

We could say that, fundamentally, spiritual awakening is 'waking up' to the spiritual nature of self and reality after 'sleeping' or being unaware of it. What the 'spiritual nature' of self and reality might be, I'll go into shortly, but awakening also means transforming into a new state of beingness, a new version of, or entirely new, self. We experience an energetic shift as our consciousness realigns to a higher frequency or vibration. It's out with the old and in with the new, meaning darker energies are purged from the self, forced out by the light of awareness we're inviting in. This purging and realigning can take us to dark places where our shadows reside and even haunt us, and this, if extreme, is called the 'dark night of the soul' (*see Chapter 3*).

We can think of awakening as the start of our spiritual journey; it's the first time we open our eyes and begin exploring a new approach to life. Throughout our journey, we continue to awaken to new possibilities, knowledge, and practices. It's like waking up in the morning; we are not waking up all day, just in the morning. But after that, we move through our day, having experiences and learning about life, sometimes 'awakening' to new possibilities. So after awakening begins, it never really ends. It tends to melt into a, hopefully, steady and level spiritual path stretching ahead, sometimes with bumps and rocky patches, other times with sunshine and roses. Perhaps the ultimate goal is enlightenment or a state of self-actualization, described by Abraham Maslow as, 'the desire for self-fulfillment, namely, to the tendency for him to become actualized in what he is potentially. This tendency might be phrased as the desire to become more and more what one is, to become everything that one is capable of becoming.'[1]

What Are We Awakening from?

Imagine you're living on an island called Accepted Thought. Everything you know and understand is on this island, and you have no idea that there is a world beyond it. Everyone else lives on the island, too, because no one ever thought to travel abroad. One day, you invent a telescope and see a vast, vivid, and inspiring world beyond the sea. Even though you're not supposed to leave, you feel an irresistible desire to do so, and decide to build a raft to explore the world beyond Accepted Thought. You, the brave explorer, learn and overcome much on the journey, and find it's not all smooth sailing, by any means, but what you find out there is rewarding and enlightening and changes your life forever.

> ❛ *An essential part of the awakening is the recognition of the unawakened you, the ego as it thinks, speaks, and acts, as well as the recognition of the collectively conditioned mental processes that perpetuate the unawakened state.* ❜
> ECKHART TOLLE

More Than a Human Being

We awaken from the illusion of our ego, which weaves itself over our true self, masking our pure, infinite, everlasting awareness. We can ask ourselves: What is this conceptual construct that I assume to be me? How did it come about, and did I choose it? Who am I? Our ego continually needs to *be* more and acquire more, but you may notice that this does not lead to happiness. We'll address this later.

Imagine looking at the world through the eyes of a person who thinks they are essentially a biological robot, blood, muscle, and bone with a computer-like brain, believing that when they're dead, they're gone. Then, see through the eyes of someone who's sure that death is not the end, that it's just a transition, and that their immortal soul consciousness is free to enjoy eternity. Imagine observing the world through both those sets of eyes, what it means and how it feels.

Once we realize we have a soul or *are* a soul, and that we experience many lifetimes, we may begin to release our fear of death at least a little, and this is very liberating. We treasure this life because a human incarnation is a tremendous catalyst for expansion and growth, and we sincerely desire to remain here with our loved ones. Still, the sense of mortality's impending doom sure puts a dampener on things, especially as we grow older. We recognize we have limited time and make the most of it, but the thought of the end is daunting for most people. Here's what it's like. If you were a kid and were taken on a fun day out but told you had to go home after half an hour, you'd be disappointed and disheartened, and would rush to have as much fun as possible. The thought of leaving would hang over you, dampening your experiences. If you were told, however, that you could stay as long as you like, you'd probably take your time, take it all in, enjoy yourself, and let loose. Likewise, as we begin to deeply grasp that the soul's nature is eternal, that our adventure never really ends, and that we can be with our loved ones literally forever, time pressures and fear of 'the end' steadily lessen.

Releasing Societal Illusions

One of the bleakest and most disheartening things I woke up from was the pressure and expectations that modern civilization had lumped upon me. I had always felt immense stress to become something more than I already was, until I learned to set my own reasonable standards and expectations. As an infinite spiritual being, how is my financial and career success a measure of who I am? The resistance to failure had been creating more failure in my life, and this was the law of attraction doing its thing as it always does. Once I released this pressure, I was finally able to create the life I wanted.

I've sprinkled this book with common and general awakening experiences gathered from clients, viewers, listeners, and course participants, and here is the first.

> *'I woke up to the fact that I was suffering endlessly and perhaps unnecessarily. Suffering was a big part of my life, happiness was fleeting, and it seemed like everyone was in the same boat. I wondered if life was supposed to be this way.'*

Suffering seems to be part of life; you need only hear a few people say that 'life is hard' to realize the general consensus and begin believing it yourself. Your thoughts and beliefs then create your reality and become compounding evidence for your belief. However, what if you can free yourself from suffering by shifting your thought patterns? We see that suffering need not be mandatory and that our ideas about life and ourselves fuel our pain. We wake up to the fact that a partner, vacation, top job, or swanky suit will not make us happy; happiness is an emotion we foster within. Problems in life are instead challenges, because they catalyze our learning, experience, and growth. We can go with the flow of the river of life instead of swimming against it and perform inner work to heal those unpleasant emotions that have been hounding us for years.

We awaken from the void within us, the empty space in our human psyche that our higher self subconsciously tells us needs filling. We understand that 'normal' life with all its rules, hierarchies, social norms, fashions, products, quick fixes, and self-serving aims, is not all there is. They are two-dimensional concepts lacking depth. There must be something more. Social status is also less appealing after awakening, because we realize we are all equal.

Wow, Consciousness Is Everywhere!

As societal illusions melt away, infinite consciousness is all that's left, presenting itself as human or even a cow, a goose, or broccoli. Okay, you probably wouldn't risk your life saving broccoli from imminent danger. Yet, we begin to understand that all beings are part of the *one* being that is Creation, just some with different levels of consciousness. All Creation is alive, including rocks, water, and air, even your shoes and dinner plate, because the same intelligent energy runs through everything.

Plants are perhaps more conscious and aware than you might think. Grover Cleveland Backster, Jr. was an expert in the use of polygraph machines. Polygraphs work by measuring physiological indicators such as pulse, respiration, and skin conductivity. One day, just for fun, Backster decided to hook up his Dracaena plant to the machine. He decided to burn one of the plant's leaves to see what would happen, but before he could do so, the polygraph registered intense reactions, similar to those of a human emotional response, coming from the plant. The Backster effect is the name given to this surprising phenomenon. His repeated tests showed that if you are going to be unkind to plants, they seem to read your mind and become upset before you even do anything. Backster also found that if you thank and have a grateful attitude toward your veggies before you eat them, they don't mind giving themselves up for your nourishment. It's fascinating how many cultures and religions encourage prayer and thanksgiving before the consumption of food; it seems we intuitively knew about plants' consciousness all along.

Realizations such as these awaken us from any disrespect we might have for animals, plants, the land, air, and sea, and instill in us a sense of sacredness toward them. It hits home that animals have souls, too, and reincarnate just as we do, evolving and progressing like us.

Beyond Material Reality

We awaken from the perspective that the physical and material is all that there is. There are highly qualified thought leaders attempting to disrupt this consensus because they, too, see past the materialist illusion. The Manifesto for a Post-Materialist Science is a set of conclusions authored by a group of eight scientists, professors, medical doctors, and thought leaders that has been signed by more than 300 similarly qualified individuals.

It states: *'We believe that the sciences are being constricted by dogmatism, and in particular by a subservience to the philosophy of materialism, the doctrine that matter is the only reality and that the mind is nothing but the physical activity of the brain.'*[2]

Upon awakening to the scientific establishment's reluctance to address phenomena outside the materialist paradigm and their shunning and ridiculing of experts who attempt to do so, we realize we are stunting our collective evolution as spiritual beings. What's stopping conventional science from taking a look at psi phenomena (mental influence at a distance), near-death experiences, remote viewing, or indeed anything spiritual in essence? Perhaps scientists are reluctant to reevaluate the established theories they've spoken about for years or don't want to appear to have been wrong. Maybe they hate to admit the existence of 'God' in any form and wish to remain at the top of their institutional hierarchies. Scientific achievements have been nothing short of miraculous, but no one should feel embarrassed to explore concepts outside of 'normal' because there are still many unanswered questions. Perhaps we will find the answers outside of 'normal,' but if we don't look, we won't find them.

What Are We Awakening to?

Spiritual awakening is a time filled with astonishment. Hooray! I love the feeling of having a profound realization. We are each, however, intrigued by different aspects of spirituality, and some realizations are more surprising than others to different people. I am particularly fascinated by the spiritual nature of reality, among other subjects, so I guess I'll start there. Here's a drop in the awakening ocean, some aspects of spirituality to which we awaken, but there's plenty more if you dive deep yourself.

The Spiritual Nature of Self and Reality

For many during awakening some of the first questions are: What is reality if it's not physical? Why are we here? What is the meaning of life? Now I don't claim to have definitive answers for you, only my research and theories to share.

> THE ALL (... all that is apparent to our material senses) is SPIRIT, which in itself is UNKNOWABLE and UNDEFINABLE, but which may be considered and thought of as AN UNIVERSAL, INFINITE, LIVING MIND.... Modern Science informs us that there is really no such thing as Matter – that what we call Matter is merely "interrupted energy or force,"... What is there then higher than Matter or Energy that we know to be existent in the Universe? LIFE AND MIND! Life and Mind in all their varying degrees of unfoldment!
>
> THE KYBALION, HERMETIC PHILOSOPHY

This quote implies that everything is *one* universal living mind. If the universe is one being, then we *are part* of that being. Not a being we might imagine to have arms, legs, and a head, but an infinite, intelligent, energetic being that is absolutely everything. Possibly God. So we realize that maybe we are part of 'God' or the 'all' and that perhaps, that being, which some also call Creation or source, is everywhere and everything. The 'all' being *spirit*, is what I meant when I mentioned the 'spiritual nature' of reality and self, itself being unknowable and undefinable.

When quantum physicists refer to matter, they actually speak of the energy of the universal, living mind. If you zoom further and further into an atom, it disappears, and what remains are waves of energy (or waves of probability). The world is far weirder on the quantum level.

> If the Zero-Point Field were included in our conception of the most fundamental nature of matter, they [scientists] realized, the very underpinning of our universe was a heaving sea of energy.
>
> LYNNE McTAGGART

Many deduce from all this that the zero-point field (also known as the unified field), the sea of energy that we call home, is actually the one being that we could call God or Creation. We exist as points of consciousness within this one being, experiencing human lifetimes seemingly separate from *each other*, but in fact we are one with everything. Oneness being all that there is.

If reality is energy, then why does it feel solid? Well, we know that our brains interpret all that we sense. Chemical and electrical signals travel from our eyes to our brain to interpret. But if our minds, our consciousnesses, are *one* with the energetic sea, continually interacting with it, we might just *think* the world 'out there' is physical and tangible when, really, it's not. It's all a matter of interpretation.

If atoms and their fundamental particles make up everything, and they are, on the smallest level, energy, then what about your body? Well, atoms are actually made up of 99.9 per cent empty space, and there's a lot of space between the atoms themselves, so your body is mostly space. How can that be? Scientists postulate that this empty space also contains a lot of energy. Researchers have discovered that DNA naturally fluoresces; in other words, our living bodily cells actually emit light. You are likely a being of pure energy. Congratulations! Do you feel like a 'light' body? Even if you don't quite yet, you can't help the true infinite energetic nature of yourself. You are amazing!

If the Universe Is One Being, What Is Its Aim?

Following is a thought process that many go through.

> *'I used to be angry that, if there was a God, they would be so cruel as to allow bad things to happen to good people. Then I realized that maybe both positive and negative experiences happen to all of us as part of our soul's journey of evolution and growth.'*

Some have concluded that if all of Creation, the universe and everything in it, is one being, then it must be existing to learn and experience itself. Creation wants to experience all that there is as it produces infinite circumstances, events, and possibilities for each organism, animal, and person. Creation is experiencing absolutely everything through each of us. On the individual level, therefore, life reveals itself to be a journey of learning and experience, as our souls reincarnate over aeons and under different circumstances, becoming ever wiser and ultimately enlightened.

Perhaps, therefore, God, Creation, source, or whichever name you prefer, is impartial about whether we have positive or negative experiences, and instead watches with interest whether we, when faced with challenges, will take positive, loving actions or negative, self-serving ones. If you think about it, in the grand scheme of things, a life of serving only the self, of gaining material possessions, money, power, or control, ultimately leads nowhere. We can only truly progress when we co-create with others for the benefit of all, and the challenge is to find our way back to the highest truth – that of love.

Empathic Awakening

When we awaken, many of us step back and look at society as a whole and see unfairness, inequality, and corruption more than we had before. We then start exploring new proposed societal structures that redress the imbalance of excessive wealth for the few and hardship for the many, and where resources are managed fairly in harmony with the Earth. As our hearts open, we genuinely feel the love in the energy of all that is, and realize that love *is* fundamental to the fabric of our reality, all else being various degrees of distortion. We begin to embody love in our approach to life, other beings, and in everything we do, because love heals, transforms, and brings out the best in everybody.

More often than not, during awakening, we also experience a flurry of empathy for others; we imagine what it's like to be in their shoes. We're starting to understand that separateness is an illusion after all.

'I always felt overwhelmed in crowds of people and thought it was social anxiety. But during my awakening, I realized it was more than that. If it was a happy occasion, I'd feel their joy, but if they were pushing and shoving to get on the train, I'd feel their frustration.'

Our empathic sense (feeling other's emotions as your own) tends to level up upon awakening. It's overwhelming for many, just like any sensory capability, and requires honing and training, and I'll explain ways to manage it later. Empathic awakening happens for a reason. Part of our evolutionary process is becoming more supportive of one another, and what better way than for us to truly understand another's feelings.

> All of mankind's inner feelings eventually manifest
> themselves as an outer reality. That applies to the
> development of cities, nations, and continents,
> as well as individuals. You don't have to become
> a great visionary – just watch the inner flow
> and you'll know what will happen next.
>
> STUART WILDE

Manifesting All the Time

The law of attraction is a fundamental law of our universe, and awakening helps us figure it out. We begin to master manifesting to create positive, sweeping change and to improve our and others' lives. Our thoughts, beliefs, and vibration have contributed to our situation and circumstances as they are now because we all manifest unconsciously until we are consciously aware of the process. Our consciousness interacts with reality because it is part of reality, and it brings us experiences based on our thoughts, beliefs, and vibrations because those are what we require for our learning and experience.

My father passed away from kidney cancer, and I miss him very much. Recently, I felt an ache in my kidney and began to worry that something was wrong. My thoughts were of kidneys; my belief was that the same thing might happen to me; and my vibration was fear. Then I started to manifest kidneys everywhere, and this was reality responding to my thoughts and feelings. A kidney disease charity flyer came in the mail, stating that 'kidney disease can happen to anyone'; my husband's friend started talking about kidney pain; and one of my kids came down with a kidney infection for the first time! (We sorted it out quickly.) I realized what was happening and meditated to release kidney-related fear, thoughts and vibrations, and the manifestations stopped. Do you see how reality responds? Imagine harnessing that power for your highest good.

Awareness of the Paranormal

Nikola Tesla is said to have stated: 'The day science begins to study non-physical phenomena, it will make more progress in one decade than in all the previous centuries of its existence.'

We awaken to the paranormal. 'Para' means 'beyond, outside of, or apart from.' So paranormal essentially means 'outside of normal,' which is a shame because the phenomena I'm about to mention happen so frequently that you could consider them normal indeed. Just a side note: Most definitions you'll find of 'paranormal' explain the 'normal' part as 'scientific understanding' or 'scientific laws.' Remember the Manifesto for a Post-Materialist Science? Enough said.

Throughout history and today, countless people tell of far-out mystical experiences, divine encounters, transformational moments, and paranormal events. Millions have been brave enough to tell their stories, but many more have not for fear of ridicule. You must know at least one person who has a tall tale to tell. Let me give you a few examples, although there are many.

If you want to read accounts of over 4,600 (at the time of this writing) near-death experiences (NDEs), the Near-Death Experience Research Foundation (nderf.org) has you covered. An NDE occurs when a person clinically dies, and they perceive themselves leaving their body and having unusual experiences. They are then revived and remember these experiences, telling of them later. To date, scientists have not been able to prove that the brain generates NDEs. Experiencers often hear and remember conversations had by the medical staff who were present with their body, or in adjacent rooms, well after brain activity had ceased. The staff have later verified the truth in the NDE experiencer's eavesdropping. There are also many commonalities in people's experiences, such as floating above the body, being greeted by family members, seeing a light or tunnel, feeling expansive, or overcome with love. Once, I read an account of a man floating above the Earth, looking down, and thinking, 'That's not the real world. This is'. My point is that, if scientists can't disprove them, can we not entertain the possibility that NDEs are actually happening and are not merely fantasies of the brain?

Throughout history, people have:

- seen ghosts, apparitions, and objects moving on their own

- experienced mediumship – the communication of messages from loved ones who have passed over, containing highly accurate information (yes there are frauds out there, but you'll know this when the reading isn't very good)

- had precognitive feelings, visions, or dreams, accurately predicting future events

- psychically read the minds of others

- performed accurate remote viewing – observing objects and places at great distances within the mind

- seen and recorded UFO phenomena (there are entire websites and YouTube channels devoted to showcasing evidence)

- had out-of-body experiences – leaving the body and moving around while unconscious (differing from NDEs because the person is very much alive)

- experienced a profound sensation of oneness with all things during meditation

- seen elementals, fairies, elves, angels, and other inter-dimensional beings of the forest, mountains, or seas

- performed telekinesis and levitation

- performed past-life regression and revisited previous lifetimes

Are all of these people mistaken or lying? Every single one? Even if only one of the paranormal experiences had by millions of people throughout history were real and genuine – just one – it would be huge! It means there *is* more to life than most people currently accept. I have a sneaky suspicion that at the very least, one is real.

Energies and Interdimensional Beings

You might wonder why UFO phenomena are part of the paranormal list. Well, this is another concept to which we awaken. If extraterrestrials exist, what else is out there? Many believe that we live lifetimes as many species, throughout the universe. As a past-life therapist, I have regressed numerous individuals to previous lifetimes as extraterrestrials, not to mention interdimensional beings existing in alternate realities and layers of existence. Some of them were so advanced that they no longer needed physical bodies and lived as pure light or energy.

We wake up to the possibility of energies and beings that we can't see but can sense, and we're likely becoming more sensitive to them. Visible light makes up only a small portion of the electromagnetic spectrum; you can't see radio waves, X-rays, or UV light, but you're told they're there. What else is there? Our human senses are tuned to our reality, like tuning a radio to a radio station. I propose that matter, too, being energy, exists at specific frequencies, and that we exist at the frequency of the universe we inhabit. I also suggest there are other layers of existence outside our frequency, and that intelligent beings live there, perhaps at different stages of evolution. Why don't we bump into entities we can't see? Because their bodies are calibrated to a different frequency of matter, yet they may share our 'space' and 'time' if such things even exist.

The Third Eye

Awakening also has a way of colorfully illustrating that we are all psychic to some degree, even if only a little. When we awaken, we begin working on improving the energy flow within our mind, body, and spirit, and attempt to clear out old energy blockages. Our third eye receives an energetic upgrade and sudden stimulation, resulting in our much-suppressed psychic abilities powerfully emerging. We may have visions, vivid dreams, and precognition, know the thoughts of others, and even experience our consciousness leaving our body. These experiences can occur involuntarily and be frightening for the unprepared. There's more on psychic abilities in Chapter 6 because they're highly significant to our evolution.

Inner Healing

Many of these concepts are a normal part of life for me now, but there's always a brand-new revelation around the corner. Often, though, contemplating our inner world teaches us the most. Awakening shows us that, through introspection and inner healing, we become more emotionally aware, resilient, even whole and complete. People's opinions of us aren't such a concern, and thoughtless comments and unreasonable behaviors trigger us less. Perhaps most importantly, once we've made progress with our inner healing, we start to find more contentment and peace.

No one can *make* you happy; it's how you *allow* yourself to feel.

We awaken to the fact that change starts within, and that if everyone began a journey of self-development and inner healing, the entire world might change for the better. Authenticity greets us with open arms – a concept that teaches us to explore and become our true self, liberating our truth and purpose.

Connection to Nature

Many of us also develop a deep connection with the natural world during awakening. Nature is Earth's default setting; we are its children; and it's our responsibility to protect it. The Earth is a living being too. Ancient ancestors and indigenous peoples might be horrified by the amount of concrete we pour over the Earth. In doing so, we insulate ourselves from Mother Nature and lose our connection. I know our vehicles would get stuck in the mud if it wasn't for all the concrete, but it's still a terrible shame.

We all gather in concrete-and-glass cities because that's where the jobs are, but numerous souls in close psychic contact tend to interfere mentally and energetically with one another. Many an empath will tell you that living in a city is exhausting, especially when exposed to unpleasant feelings coming from others. Do you have a grumpy coworker or neighbor? That's a real challenge for an empath. Without the resetting and balancing powers of nature, psychic interference can accumulate. The natural world absorbs and transmutes unpleasant energies, so it's essential to get out among the trees and grass as often as possible.

Waking Up to Now

We awaken to a fascination with the intricacies and beauty of life, and the present moment. I always observe how others seem to exhibit displeasure at the present moment, as if 'now' is never good enough and must be enhanced by the next distraction or aim. Happiness is never *now* because we chase it as if it exists on some far horizon if we could only do more or something else to get there. But if we do reach that horizon, a new one soon presents itself. Spirituality grants us permission to stop and observe the beauty in the world, and surprisingly, wonders and enjoyment are abundant in even the littlest things. The smell in the air after summer rain, the smile of a loved one, the freshness of a spring morning accompanied by a blackbird's song – all things often present but that escape our awareness. Lost in our thoughts or caring about our far horizons, we miss the wonders of the miracle of existence – no more of this blindness upon awakening.

> *'During my awakening, I began noticing little things I'd been ignoring. On my walk to work, I became aware of the wind in the trees, amazing talent in some graffiti, and the joy in the laughter of kids as they made their way to school. I've been immersed in an endless stream of thoughts for so long, that when I opened my eyes and actually observed the world, it really hit me how miraculous and beautiful it is. I saw perfection even in the imperfect.'*

What a treasure it is to awaken to meditation, one of the most profound tools we have for spiritual growth in every way imaginable. Not only does meditation provide the opportunity for finding peace and balance, but it also enhances our connection with the divine and allows us to explore our inner world.

In combination with inner-work healing, meditation opens doors to inflowing high vibrational energy, wisdom, foresight, and infinite awareness. Before we awaken, most of us are unable to turn and face infinity; we are looking down, keeping limited, the 'veil' is over our head. Once spiritual wisdom and love-light energy enter our frame of reference, we have the opportunity to go deeply inward and heal. Our consciousness advances in leaps and bounds along the road of transformation if we first clear all the unwanted stuff out of our heavy, old backpack. Inner work and meditation help facilitate this.

Why Does Spiritual Awakening Happen?

Seeing as we are soul consciousness, we each must know, on some level, that standard, earthly, day-to-day life is not a universal model. Consciousness, by its very nature, wants growth, free will, and experience, and so constant monotony, although an experience in itself, is not usually satisfactory and is definitely not the point of existence. Past-life regression accounts tell of other planets and civilizations where inhabitants enjoy harmonious, heart-led lives. So deep down, many of us feel that earthly life has the potential for much improvement, and perhaps we awaken because higher aspects of ourselves know we can do something about it.

Subconscious remembering is stronger for some than others, but some people don't seem to have much at all. We receive a memory block at birth, and this happens for good reasons. Imagine a child who has full recollection of lives between lives, of universal truths, of psychic abilities, how to read minds, move objects via thought, and manifest instantly, right in front of them, anything they desire. Such powers would seem godlike to everyone else. Additionally, the child might remember previous human lifetimes and begin searching for their former family, or perhaps hold a grudge against a 16th-century warlord and bravely head out to hunt them down. They might recall and be traumatized by their last passing.

Perhaps spiritual awakening occurs because, on an individual soul level, we have chosen to spend part of our life under earthly illusions and conditioning, and the rest of it liberated and motivated to find our way back to an authentic expression of ourselves. We learn what it's like to live under both circumstances, and this is perhaps part of the purpose of our incarnation. It's a puzzle set by our higher self for us to figure out. What a fascinating adventure for our higher self to observe!

We might, therefore, have chosen before birth to awaken at a certain point in our life when we have gained enough experience to be able to help and assist others after our own awakening. I know that the life experiences I had before my transformation have helped me immensely to understand, empathize with, and serve others. So I was meant to awaken when I did, and my higher self knows that too.

Awakenings might be happening more frequently these days because, on a mass psychic level, we cannot hide spiritual revelations from one another. Each of us has a subconscious connection to the collective consciousness of humanity, even though most of us don't realize it. There is evidence of our collective consciousness too. Two or more people have invented or discovered the same thing at the same time on numerous occasions throughout history, even though they had no contact with each other. For example, calculus, the telephone, and jet engines were invented by more than one person around the same time period. Does this mean that ideas are floating around and formulating within our mass-mind for anyone to access? I believe all kinds of ideas are out there, waiting to be shared.

The Global Consciousness Project monitors a set of around 70 random number generators (RNGs) located around the world. They have found that when a significant global event occurs, especially one that produces elevated emotions, the output of the number generators sometimes alters. Instead of generating random numbers, generators begin to show significant patterns.

> *When a great event synchronizes the feelings of millions of people, our network of RNGs becomes subtly structured. We calculate one in a trillion odds that the effect is due to chance. The evidence suggests an emerging noosphere or the unifying field of consciousness described by sages in all cultures.*
> THE GLOBAL CONSCIOUSNESS PROJECT

If our collectively focused thoughts and emotions have such a profound effect, imagine what we could achieve together if we focus our usually scattered attention toward meaningful goals. So if our collective consciousness is the reason for so many awakenings happening, and the few are causing the many to awaken, then we seem to be observing a natural, collective shift in consciousness. As soon as a triggering event occurs for an individual, the collective consciousness is standing by, subconsciously offering spiritual wisdom. It's been there all along, we simply open our mental doors to it.

We can also ask: Why doesn't everyone awaken? Perhaps some people are not paying attention to their subconscious remembering or are purposefully ignoring it. Maybe their higher self doesn't want them to awaken during their current lifetime, or perhaps they will, but aren't ready to do so yet.

I call the subconscious mind 'the bridge to the soul' because when we relax, it becomes dominant over our conscious mind, and it's during these times that we access our clairvoyance and intuition most effectively. Hypnosis is all about working with the subconscious mind. In practicing past-life regression hypnosis, I've found that those who have difficulty relaxing and focusing their awareness inward block out higher aspects of self. Therefore, those who are continuously absorbed in earthly distractions or lost in ever-whirring thoughts and worries are unlikely to have clear access to the wisdom of their higher self. This could be the reason why many people *don't* awaken – their minds are simply too noisy to hear their inner wisdom.

Some people actively reject spiritual and metaphysical concepts because they have the potential to chip away at their existing paradigm in which they feel safe. It doesn't mean they are not lovely people. A well-meaning doctor might be reluctant to entertain the prospect of effective alternative, holistic healing methods for fear of negating and invalidating his or her years of establishment-approved medical training and practice.

Many believe that the Earth is making a transition. The best psychics and channelers have been speaking of this for years. They say that the Earth is moving into a new dimension of existence, a higher frequency of energy/matter, and the vibration of this new Earth will be closer to that of love. If this is the case – and I intuitively believe it is – then this new earthly vibration may be initiating awakenings all over the world. As the Earth levels up, spiritually speaking, so do we.

Now that we've thought about why awakening happens, let's see *how* it happens. Some of what follows might be very similar to your own experiences.

Chapter 2

Causes of Spiritual Awakening

Often, a little prod is all that's needed to initiate awakening. Sometimes, though, it's a big, forceful shove. Our latent potential for awakening can't always expand on its own, and a causal event is needed to get the process going. But why is this?

Consider a bird in a cage that cannot fly until the door opens. Until then, the bird stays as it is. It has all the potential to soar high and free but cannot. It's only when the moment of change occurs, the momentous event when the door swings open, that the bird can stretch its wings and go wherever it wants.

In this section, I describe those who experience awakening caused by significant events or circumstances. But we mustn't forget – and this might apply to you – that some people awaken gradually over time with no big bang, no breaking down or building back up. They simply go about exploring their inner world and spiritual wisdom at their own pace. The causal or triggering event, however, is the tipping point for many.

Before awakening, you may have heard tidbits of spiritual ideas over time, perhaps from friends or media, but those ideas never really made much of a difference to you. You might have encountered the paranormal, perhaps something weird or unexplained happened, but still, it didn't trigger your awakening. Maybe you saw an advertisement about meditation and its transformative power or watched a documentary about spiritually connected indigenous peoples, but still, none of it hit home or really moved you. But then, a triggering event occurs, that last weight added to the scales that shifts the balance toward awakening, a piece of definitive evidence, one final realization that overloads the pressure on your consciousness to search for answers. And now you have endless questions!

Awakening is something that happens within you and not out there. Still, it can be triggered by something external to you. The trigger takes you beyond the limit of being able to ignore what you've been overlooking. It's a shift in your psyche that forces itself upon you. Like many, you don't ask for it. You can feel like you're losing control, like being in a racing car accelerating to top speed, the brakes aren't working, and you're unable to stop.

I've split the causes or triggers of awakening into six possibilities: a sudden event, ongoing circumstances, a paranormal event, acquiring information, meditative experiences, and psychedelics. Each has the potential to initiate awakening. It is fascinating how there are different routes toward the same destination. One of them may have formed part of your story.

A Sudden Event

This category is all about suddenness, a shocking or traumatic unforeseen event that blows your life to bits. It's like you're a piece of glass shattering on the floor.

> *'I felt like I was collapsing inward. My father and sister passed away within a year, and everything changed. I sank into depression and really couldn't get any lower, then I started to question the point of life. This experience led me to search for ways to heal, to find new meaning, and to find out if my loved ones were really gone forever.'*

Many of us simply don't have the mental or emotional tools to deal with sudden traumatic events, and we find ourselves unable to cope with our usual responsibilities and other people. Life becomes impossible to manage, and anxiety, guilt, and sadness can take hold, making it tough to function. The sudden event is a very common trigger of spiritual awakening because sometimes we need to sink low before we can transform.

When my relationship broke down, and I moved to a new town with my children, I lost the life I knew and began building a new one, alone. There was a lot to organize, and I was severely overloaded. Even the smallest problems would cause anxieties, and they mounted up. I also felt tremendous guilt toward my children; although I knew this path was for the best, and it took great courage to initiate it, I still worried about them. My kids thought it was all an exciting adventure and loved their new school, so they were fine; I was the one who was struggling.

The crushing embarrassment of failure and the feeling that I was useless stuck me like a knife every day. I was utterly defeated.

There was an overdue debt from the previous occupants of our home, and the utility provider was trying to get the money out of me. I didn't have it of course, and this and other problems resulted in my sinking into depression. I still put on a happy face for the kids, even though the heating didn't work, the windows were leaky, and it was snowing outside. I had one family member nearby, and they were terrific, but I'd always been reluctant to ask anyone for help. The sheer hopelessness of the situation triggered memories of the concepts I used to love as I desperately searched for some light in the darkness. I went to YouTube and searched for 'consciousness,' and up popped a list of videos that I began to surf. Knowledge began to flow into my own consciousness and realizations came rapidly. I quickly began to search for truth from many different sources, on- and off-line, and from within myself. A little like Alice, on her exciting and curious adventure into Wonderland, down the rabbit hole I went into an entirely new world.

When things can't get any worse, we allow ourselves to try something new. Well, why not? Nothing else is working. We become open to avenues of thought we'd never usually entertain, perhaps to the unconventional and unusual. When this actually works, makes sense, and we begin to feel better, we realize we've found some truth. Many might turn to drink or drugs to mask the pain of sudden trauma, but these don't offer ways to heal or roads to hope like conscious and mind-expanding knowledge can.

When we feel vulnerable, we need tools that help us help ourselves. Often, the best ones nurture our strength and our ability to transcend ordeals, assisting us to deal with emotions such as grief, sadness, and despair, not the ones that mask or avoid them. Upon awakening, we learn to listen to and sit with our feelings and not to resist them; we go inward and work with our energies to heal and find peace and stability.

Facing death – another sudden event – is undoubtedly a wake-up call. When this happens, it becomes very apparent that we've been sleeping our life away, just going along with our usual behaviors and whatever assumptions we've made.

'I was driving, and a car pulled out in front of me. I swerved to avoid it and hit a sloping verge. As my car rolled over and over, time slowed down. I saw my family in my mind and felt the pain of never seeing them again. My purpose also came into question, as I realized there was much I wanted to do but might not get the chance. I felt regret that maybe I hadn't made the most of my life, and now it was going to be cut short. I survived, but at that moment, everything changed. I had to find the purpose and meaning I was lacking.'

Further examples of sudden causes of spiritual awakening are:

- loss of job, home, or a loved one

- change in circumstances (such as moving home, finishing college, traveling)

- an accident

- a violent incident (such as robbery or attack)

- witnessing death

- a medical diagnosis

- a midlife crisis

- war, rebellion, shortage of resources, or other countrywide or global events

- natural disasters (such as hurricane or flood)

- working in an occupation involving traumatic circumstances (such as the military, health service, or aid work)

- witnessing any of the above happen to others or supporting them through it

Such events lead us to search for support and guidance from reliable sources, in whatever form they present themselves. Nowadays, the prevalence of books, videos, audio recordings, and articles on topics such as personal development, well-being, and spirituality, provides easy access not just to comfort and reassurance, but also to healing methods and constructive ways forward. The book you are reading right now exists to do just that. Therefore, today, many more people can improve their own mental and emotional well-being and feel empowered to do so.

A sudden life-changing, negative-feeling event can cause our ego to start melting away. I'll explain ego dissolution soon, but the trigger is just the start of it. Like an ice sculpture in sub-zero temperatures, the ego will persist in the right conditions indefinitely. But when things suddenly heat up, the ice sculpture melts. This is the beginning of the end for the ego. The construct of 'you,' the concept of who or what you believe you are, can't always withstand the destructive power of shock or trauma. If your ego breaks down, it leaves you with a lack of identity, and you'll likely find yourself searching and seeking for ways to fill that void. Many find that spiritual and conscious concepts help them reinvent themselves into new stronger, wiser, and calmer versions of themselves, better able to deal with other sudden events should they come along in the future.

Ongoing Circumstances

Trying to maintain an inauthentic version of yourself is pretty exhausting, especially when your daily activities feel unauthentic or detrimental to your well-being. At some point, the house of cards comes tumbling down because, in time, it's become increasingly unstable.

Ongoing unfavorable or unpleasant circumstances take their toll on the psyche, and due to consciousness's quest for growth and experience, sooner or later, your authentic self tries to break free. Consciousness seeks to evolve, progress, expand, and grow; it dislikes restriction or imprisonment. Have you ever been stuck in a job you disliked? Every occupation is repetitive to some degree, but was there a lack of stimulation, fair reward, interest, or overriding benefit to the world? Mind or consciousness seems equipped to endure only a finite duration of captivity before it says, 'I've had enough!' Your soul knows there is more to life, and times of rebellion are symptoms of this knowing seeping through.

> *For most people, their spiritual teacher is their suffering.*
> *Because eventually the suffering brings about awakening.*
> ECKHART TOLLE

Like a rubber band stretched to its absolute limit, your patience and endurance will snap sooner or later, and although a relief, it can be rather painful. Bravery is required, but often we get to the point where fearlessness naturally arises because the instinct for self-preservation overrides our desire to fit in or conform.

'My work was so stressful that my health was failing. I had constant fatigue, aching muscles, and nausea. The pressure to get everything done was crushing, and nobody ever seemed to notice my hard work. I always wanted to travel the world, but after my bills were paid, there was nothing left over. I wondered if this was how life was supposed to be. The day came when I couldn't take it anymore, and I quit my job so dramatically, it was like I was possessed! Afterward, I felt embarrassed and irresponsible, but now that I'm doing what I love in life, I'm pleased I did what I did.'

Now, I'm not recommending you quit your job in a blaze of glory; it's always best to make sure you'll be provided for first. But I've spoken to hundreds of people who did just that. Although you're not actually possessed, it can feel like a strong and willful part of you is stepping forward to fix the situation. This is your subconscious mind acting on behalf of higher aspects of yourself to free your mind and liberate your potentials. If we never make new memories, relentless repetition grows tiresome. If we feel our actions have no overriding benefit to others or the world, we can become swamped in meaninglessness. The search for meaning begins.

> *'I suffered from bouts of deep sadness for most of my life and was seeing a counselor. She was great, but still, things got increasingly worse until I had a total breakdown. That's when things changed. I knew that if I went on like this, I wouldn't survive. My friend offered to take me along to her yoga class, and although I thought it was a waste of time, I dragged myself out. It was the yoga teacher who recommended teachings to help me. They gave me hope, and I was finally able to begin healing the causes of my sadness, which began when I was younger. I still do yoga today because I feel more peace when I'm doing that than I've ever felt before.'*

Every unpleasant emotion is a sign from our subconscious mind that something requires attention within. Our subconscious mind often cries out for healing, and that's why we should accept and sit with our emotions and listen to them. The aforementioned case illustrates how unpleasant feelings can continually emerge when circumstances and events from the past remain unaddressed. Once we've experienced the symptoms of unhealed trauma long enough, there'll come a point where consciousness automatically takes a new approach for the sake of self-preservation.

> *'Both my son and my partner have chronic health conditions, and I am their full-time caregiver. I love them more than anything, but the guilt and worry that I wasn't doing enough for them, and the amount of work I had to do every day, led me to experience extreme burnout. Something snapped in my mind, and I began exploring ways to take care of myself emotionally and spiritually to avoid experiencing burnout again. I managed to bring my life into perspective.'*

When day-to-day circumstances cause continual guilt, worry, fear, or other unpleasant emotions, we find ourselves caught in a negative vibratory loop. Daily painful feelings bathe everything in dim light. We can only do the best that we can, but there are times when we don't give ourselves credit for our efforts, especially when they involve the people we love and their well-being. Sometimes there is no way out of a situation – we have responsibilities that we must, and actually want to, fulfill. But in those cases, a new approach with fresh perceptions can significantly reduce physical and emotional suffering.

Other ongoing circumstances that can trigger awakening are:

◉   hopelessness and futility

◉   lack of fulfillment

◉   lack of direction

◉   boredom

◉   chronic mental health conditions

- ⊚ chronic illness

- ⊚ drinking and drug use

- ⊚ repression of true sexuality or gender

- ⊚ bullying and violence

- ⊚ stress and trauma

- ⊚ psychic or empathic interference

- ⊚ negative, restrictive, or dangerous circumstances

You may have searched for happiness in the same fruitless places for a long time, so the moment your mind changes or rebels can feel liberating and relieving. Your true, infinite, immortal self has had enough of feeling invalidated. Yet very often, there are elements of fear. Although the circumstances leading to your rebellion of consciousness have been ongoing, the rebellion itself is usually sudden, and uncertainty and vulnerability set in. For many people, the shock stage of awakening begins at this point, followed by the searching and seeking for information stage. (*See also Chapter 3.*)

A Paranormal Event

When we witness a paranormal event, we are powerfully forced to observe the metaphysical nature of reality, and this has the potential to trigger awakening. After a lifetime of believing the established consensus of how reality works, we are shown a version to the contrary. Many people rationalize their experiences, and it's true, some *are* due to imagination, tricks of light, or mistakes, but some are not. Sometimes there is no rational explanation. A paranormal event is a trigger for awakening because it suddenly opens our eyes to the unknown, providing irrefutable personal evidence of real phenomena, beings, or energies that 'shouldn't' exist. Now we have a story of our own to tell, rather than only hearing the unproven stories of others, and the frustrating thing is, we can't prove our story to others either.

Sometimes several paranormal events are required to initiate full transformational awakening. We can remain in the 'that was weird' frame of mind for years and not take spiritual exploration much further. As the experiences mount up, though, and proof accumulates, there'll come the point where the evidence can't be ignored.

Once, I unmistakably witnessed an earthbound spirit at the same moment as someone else. We both saw an apparition as clear as day. Although this event didn't catalyze my full-blown awakening, it did confirm for me the continuance of life or at least our ability to peer into unknown realities. Such an experience ultimately added weight to my eventual awakening, resulting in my exploring spirituality during my traumatic event, instead of remaining in depression.

At age 18, I was watching a movie in my room with my then-boyfriend. We were sitting on chairs set side by side. As the movie finished, we both happened to glance across the room and saw a cat on the bed. Now, my family no longer owned a cat, so this did seem rather peculiar. Stranger still was the cat's partial transparency. A moment later, it jumped off the bed and ran under my chair. Absolutely flabbergasted, I turned to my boyfriend and asked, 'Did you see that?' 'Yes,' he replied, his face turning pale. 'A gray-and-white cat with its tail pointing upward? It ran under your chair!' We looked around, and the cat was gone.

There were no possible light sources from outside to create a trick of the light, and even so, both the blinds and the curtains were closed. Intriguingly, the ghostly apparition looked exactly like our cat that had died about five years previously. It had the same patterns on its coat, only in life they had been black and white not gray and white, which perhaps was owing to its new partially see-through appearance. I saw the cat a few times again over the following years. Once, running down the corridor toward my room, and once again, in the living room. But to see an unmistakable apparition at the same time as someone else proved to me that it wasn't my imagination. My ex-boyfriend mentioned it to me again after I hadn't seen him in a long time (the cat wasn't the reason we broke up!), and he mentioned that it had affected him significantly too. It hadn't sent him into an awakening, but it had changed his perceptions of life, and he had clearly been reflecting on it for years.

This kind of 'outside of normal' experience changes you at least a little bit because it has far-reaching implications about the nature of life. Earlier, I listed a plethora of paranormal experiences such as NDEs, visions, and UFO sightings, and any of these are transformational enough to penetrate the veil of forgetting and initiate a spiritual awakening.

'I had a vivid dream that I was walking my dog through the woodland near my home as I always do. I decided to take a new route that led me over a hilltop overlooking a busy road. As I walked over the hill, I glanced toward the overpass. Just then, a car on the bridge hit another car, and another swerved to avoid the accident. As it did, it careered through the barrier, fell, and hit the road below. I suddenly became aware that I was dreaming and woke up shaking. Two weeks later, my friend's wife called to inform me that my friend had passed away in an accident just a couple of days before. Utterly devastated, I asked her what had happened. Although she hadn't been with him, the events she described matched my dream exactly. He had been in the car that fell from the overpass onto the road below. Not only did my friend's passing hugely affect me, but witnessing it in my dream before it happened also shocked me in a way that I just can't describe.'

This is based on a real experience one of my family members had. How could he have known what would happen? What are the chances of having such a specific dream before the very same event? Perhaps one in a billion? If we can view the future of someone we love and be there as if it were happening in the now, maybe this means the future is written unless we take action to change it. Or perhaps our loved ones who have passed over still exist and can show us future events. Can we, therefore, see the future if we learn how?

Do you see how many questions such an event can pose? Awakening can ensue as a result of needing those questions answered to feel settled in a newly mysterious reality. The unknown can be frightening because we don't know what else to expect and prepare for.

The first reading I had with a spirit medium was an absolute corker and changed my perception of everything. It was one of the events that compounded my eventual awakening; this medium was the real deal. She didn't know me or anything about me, yet was on point with everything she said. As the reading began, I was a little surprised when a golden strand of energy came down and entered my body, but I just thought, *That was weird*, and carried on. She told me she had my grandmother (Nanna) with her, and that she had died at age 97 the previous October. She said that Nanna was laughing and saying that she had nearly made it to 100 years old, just as her own mother had. Okay, that got my attention. It was all true, and Nanna did use to joke that she was trying to reach 100, as her mother did. The medium proceeded to name my sisters; how my grandfather, aunt, and uncle had passed away; and asked me to give a message to my dad (still alive at the time). She said to tell him not to feel sad that he didn't reach his sister overseas before she passed away. This was something my dad had deeply regretted, and at this point, I began to cry. Even though it was a telephone reading, the medium was able to tell me I was pregnant, which I was, and that the child would be born almost two weeks early, which turned out to be true. Among numerous other pieces of validation, she finished up by saying that, although I had Nanna's necklace, there were earrings to go with it, which I should have been given. I said I didn't think there were earrings, but okay. The reading ended, and I was immensely thankful to her. Next time I visited my parents, even though I'd told them nothing about the reading, Mum promptly presented me with the pair of matching earrings. I gave Dad the message, and although he didn't like to admit he believed in such things, he was visibly surprised and moved. It was great healing for him.

Such paranormal experiences can be breathtakingly beautiful as they introduce you to another world. I can't describe how wonderful it felt to have personal proof that Nanna was still around and to know that my loved ones are always looking out for me. It opened a whole new dimension to life, one that I'll remain connected with forever.

Information to Blow Your Mind

As simple as finding something out, awakening can begin to take you. However, it's rare to be told one fascinating tidbit of knowledge and then find yourself on the path of searching and seeking. You might need to learn several concepts that stimulate your interest or receive personal proof first. Occasionally, though, one profound piece of information is all that's required to trigger the urge to dig deeper.

'A friend told me that back in the 1970s and 80s, research on remote viewing and psychic abilities was more commonplace and less taboo than now. Researchers in universities and other centers consistently found robust evidence for precognition, non-local perception, and mind-to-mind communication. Some of the work was even done for intelligence agencies. Physicist Russell Targ was one such researcher, and reading about his work really opened my eyes. What does this mean for us? And why is it not common knowledge?'

The first fragment of information you come upon can lead to more and more, as if you are intentionally being guided through a series of concepts that you're supposed to learn at that time. They all come together like pieces of a puzzle to form a broader picture of the spiritual nature of self and reality. Information can find you through word of mouth, books, magazines, online media, and social media, and it doesn't have to be spiritual or conscious in nature, but merely a mention of something that contradicts your version of reality or creates an urge to find out more. Word of mouth is one of the most significant sources of information to trigger awakening. Perhaps someone you know told you something that awakened you. Maybe you carried that thought with you for a long time before it made any difference.

The term *conspiracy theorist* is prevalent nowadays and is often used as a derogatory term, even when someone is questioning authority or seeking the truth. It's ridiculous to assume that corruption and manipulation do not exist in society, and many such theories may indeed hold water. Some we see unfolding, and others have been proven true. The prevalence of such theories causes many to look into them further to make up their own minds. Conspiracy theories, the factual ones, can connect the dots for many people about why life is as it is, and therefore, awakening can follow. They are a route to awakening. People discover, among other things, that (potentially):

- Ancient (possibly sinister) wisdom is covertly used to control the masses.

- Our true spiritual nature and abilities are hidden from us to keep us subdued within the current societal paradigm and to prevent our evolution.

- New technologies that could free humanity are being suppressed to preserve the current balance of wealth and power.

- The existence of extraterrestrials has been known to 'hidden governments' for years.

- Certain global events are not what they seem and are orchestrated to implement greater surveillance and control.

- A small group of powerful elites controls most or all governments and has the ultimate aim of achieving a global dictatorship or 'new world order.'

These possibilities have spiritual consequences, and if true, should be known, and action should be taken. But becoming aware of such information can send us down a dark, bitter path of awakening for a while. I'm not saying this happens to everybody, especially if they balance this information with more optimistic teachings. But I've seen it many times.

Meditative Experience

We don't necessarily need information from external sources to awaken us, because we have innate knowledge and wisdom within. Meditation is a powerful tool for connecting us with the higher aspects of self so that we can retrieve our universal understanding. It allows us to take the perspective of infinite awareness rather than that of our individual roles, such as Ryan, the insurance salesman, or Molly, the accountant. Meditation changes our brain chemistry by giving us a break from being perpetually lost in thought, and provides our consciousness with peacefulness training, which we can carry through into daily life.

Many believe they have journeyed to Earth to bring certain vital concepts into this reality. They are born, grow up, and remember spiritual concepts that they must verbalize and convey to those in need or who are suffering from the 'human condition.' They are messengers. Meditation can facilitate access to such wisdom, and, perhaps because of this, we have the intuitive urge to do it. Maybe our higher self is quietly compelling us to meditate. Another thing that meditation – or at least a relaxed meditative state – can reveal to us is our ability to transcend the confines of the self, our personality, and body.

> *'I was sitting in my favorite place under a tree by the stream. I closed my eyes and focused my attention on the sound of the running water. No thoughts came to me for a long time because I was completely tuned in to my surroundings, and it was beautiful. The sound of the stream began to overcome me, and I became conscious of my own awareness as if I were only awareness and nothing else. Then I became the stream, and then the tree, the grass, pebbles, air, and the birds in the sky. I was all of them. I felt large and expansive as my awareness merged with everything around me. I was at peace, one with all, and although this has not happened since, I now know that this feeling exists and that it holds profound meaning.'*

I'm always amazed by the number of people who tell of this kind of experience, and I've had it too. The commonalities are incredible, and it's the same story over and over. They say they were sitting or walking mindfully or performing meditation when they suddenly realized they are one with all things. They know it so deeply that there is simply no doubt. It is often enough firsthand, personal proof of the divinity and unity of all things that it initiates spiritual awakening. It could be classed as a paranormal experience, but it happens so often to people that I'm sure it's becoming normal. It's referred to as *samadhi*.

Samadhi is the complete state; the fulfilled state of mind. And you will find many, many different ideas among the sects of Buddhists and Hindus as to what samadhi is. Some people call it a trance, some people call it a state of consciousness without anything in it; knowing with no object of knowledge. Some people say that it is the unification of the knower and the known.

ALAN WATTS

I believe anyone can experience *samadhi* if they meditate with no expectation of anything happening and practice quietening the mind while tuning in to their awareness of the present moment. Then, and often just for a moment, their vibration rises just enough to experience an expansive, psychic connection with all that there is, accompanied by feelings of bliss and joy, as they genuinely understand that they are one with the all.

Many meditators use their practice as a means for achieving calmness without believing in anything spiritual or metaphysical. Meditation can be performed for many years without it initiating any kind of significant spiritual transformation. But suddenly and unexpectedly, phenomena can occur during meditative states of consciousness, such as visions, precognition, or energetic movement. This can be rather a surprise for the nonspiritual meditator and may even initiate their awakening. In the right state of mind and high vibration, consciousness can naturally awaken on its own with no external stimuli whatsoever.

Psychedelics

Psychedelic substances undoubtedly have the potential to trigger spiritual awakening and frequently do. I'm not encouraging or recommending anything, just pointing this out.

Mother Earth offers the potential for awakening, for those who are ready, through many types of plants growing all over the world. Psilocybin mushrooms are known to help people have profound realizations, to experience the interconnectedness of all things, and to cause the ego to melt away. There can be a dissolving of the self as if there is no I, and from this perspective, we recognize the illusions we have been under. Many also say that the mushrooms speak to them.

LSD, a semisynthetic compound with a similar molecular structure to psilocybin mushrooms, has comparable effects but with a different feel and duration of experience. Under its influence, people can have far-out visuals and visions. Again, there may be a state of having no self, a dissolution of the ego, which can be quite traumatic, especially for the unprepared. Many have carelessly taken a sizable dose of psilocybin or LSD at a public event, only to find themselves having a 'bad trip' and absolutely freaking out. I witnessed this myself when I was younger and felt their fear. Interestingly, many people while tripping together actually have shared experiences, see the same visions, and have similar realizations. This suggests the possibility of some occurrences being more real than imaginary.

Psychedelics should be treated with the respect they deserve and not be taken lightly. Treated as a sacred experience, ceremonial if possible, psychedelics have the potential to uncover the darkest aspects of your psyche, and dramatically and immersively bring them to your attention for healing. Likewise, illuminating and transformational experiences occur, ones that show us perceptions of life that our human ego would never allow us to see.

'I had a small dose of mushrooms, and my body began to feel really heavy. My friend was there to take care of me. I decided to go upstairs and look in the mirror, and I had the craziest experience of my life. I recognized myself, and yet it was like meeting myself for the first time. I thought, Oh, you seem like a great person. I then realized how I've always felt negatively about myself every time I look in the mirror – frustration that I wasn't doing enough, that I wasn't good enough, constant disappointment, and that I was a little overweight. But all that vanished. Every single perception and limiting belief about myself was gone, and I saw myself with fresh eyes, totally anew. What I saw was pretty good, and considerably improved my self-esteem. I had never realized that my perception of self was so distorted, because it was just normal for me. But once it was removed for a few moments, I was able to question my negative perceptions and release them.'

Here the human ego disappeared for a while, allowing the experiencer to meet themselves as if for the first time and judge themselves like anyone would judge someone they just met. This person judged themselves in a very positive light when otherwise they wouldn't have. This is the kind of transformational experience that can occur. It can be challenging to identify our shadow sometimes, but such substances can present a shortcut to clearing it away. If you're strong enough to handle the truth, of course, long-held perceptions are removed where otherwise they never would be, revealing a new version of self or reality. In addition to this, psychedelics are known to cause spontaneous kundalini awakening (*see Chapter 6*) and sudden moments of enlightenment.

I must reiterate that psychedelic experiences can sometimes take a dark turn, and one must be prepared to potentially relive highly traumatic events from the past or hateful feelings about the self if they exist. Sometimes we don't realize such negativities exist. Psychedelics, especially ayahuasca, have a way of bringing up what needs healing the most, and depending on the dosage, cause us to experience it to a greater or lesser degree. You can end up reliving the worst times of your life that you've buried deeply for your emotional protection. In being forced to face them, you can heal, but in some cases, unsettle yourself more until you can reconcile with them.

> *All political leaders should be obliged to go through ten Ayahuasca sessions before being admitted to office.*
> Graham Hancock

Ayahuasca ceremonies are popular nowadays, and seekers journey to retreats in Peru or Costa Rica, for example, to experience deep healing and purging. These retreats are popular because of the profound mental, emotional, and spiritual transformation people experience during the ceremonies. Participants often need considerable time to reflect upon, understand, and integrate their experiences, and are frequently in surprise and awe at what the powerful plant healer has shown them about themselves. If we don't know what needs healing, how can we heal? This is why spiritual seekers are interested in ayahuasca – the spiritual path is one of great healing.

To the one who has not yet experienced spiritual awakening by any measure, a psychedelic experience can be a real eye opener, perhaps even a third-eye or heart opener. Some might take psychedelics just for the experience or because friends are doing it, but frequently they come away not just thinking, *That was weird,* but also more like, *What the hell just happened to me?* They have an experience so far-out, so intense and transformational, that they're catapulted onto the path of awakening.

Another naturally occurring chemical substance, DMT (short for N, N-Dimethyltryptamine) is present in psychedelics such as ayahuasca, but utilized on its own is different. It provides more of an experiential adventure – people have reported meeting spirits and extraterrestrials, visiting far-off worlds and dimensions, and witnessing all kinds of incredible phenomena in the room around them, such as seeing through their own hands or observing friends' eyes becoming big and alien-like. DMT experiences can be overwhelming and frightening for some, and not conducive to a peaceful state of mind. But for others, the discovery of otherworldly beings and places seemingly 'realer than real' leads them to start questioning their previously held beliefs about what *is* even real. They ask, 'How can that be? What *was* that?'

> *'I laid my head back and felt time melt away. I can't convey how this actually felt, because I can't quite conceptualize it now. But I know I experienced a sense of timelessness, realizing that time is utterly illusory and doesn't really exist. I felt it – I actually felt it. Then as I closed my eyes, I was somewhere else. It seemed like a Mayan civilization, but not ancient; it was modern, somewhere far from Earth. There were structures with symbols all over them, and beings and animals dancing and welcoming me forward. They were wise, advanced, and pretty intense.'*

When we experience something outside the realm of imagination or impossible to ever dream up, we start suspecting it came from elsewhere. If our individual consciousness is one with the all, then perhaps psychedelics have the ability to dissolve the barriers surrounding our human psyche, allowing our awareness to spread out and voyage to distant corners of the universe. New possibilities open up outside the human experience. Many believe that authorities don't want us to have such mind-expanding experiences because we might evolve beyond current societal illusions, beyond being governed by the existing paradigm.

> *Psychedelics are illegal not because a loving government is concerned that you might jump out of a third-story window. Psychedelics are illegal because they dissolve opinion structure and culturally laid-down models of behavior and information processing. They open you up to the possibility that everything you know is wrong.*
>
> TERENCE MCKENNA

In weighing the healing and experiential benefits of psychedelics against their potential for misuse and harm, perhaps society can find a new balance and use them as Mother Earth perhaps intended. Given their profound effects as experienced by many people, psychedelics may well exist for a reason.

So, the cause or trigger of your awakening has happened. Now what? Let's see.

~

Chapter 3

Deconstruction Stages of Awakening

The stages of awakening are different for everybody and can happen in various orders with diverse intensities and time scales. They tend to start out in dark and challenging ways and become increasingly positive and enjoyable as more light enters your life. Some experience a wonderfully joyous time, though, existing in states of love and bliss, delighted to be releasing their earthly illusions. Others have a more shocking and turbulent ride or a mixture of highs and lows.

The term *spiritual emergency* is often aptly used to describe the state of intense emotional, mental, and spiritual crisis that some enter upon awakening.

> *Many episodes of unusual states of mind, even those that are dramatic and reach psychotic proportions, are not necessarily symptoms of disease in the medical sense.*

We view them as crises of the evolution of consciousness, or "spiritual emergencies," comparable to the states described by the various mystical traditions of the world.

STANISLAV GROF AND CHRISTINA GROF

The term has a dual meaning in that the suddenness of the transformation feels like an emergency, and emergencies imply danger and seriousness. Although we are unlikely to be in actual danger, it can feel that way. The other facet to the meaning is that awakening is also a time of emergence – emerging from the old self into the new.

The stages of awakening happen for a reason; you're working toward transcending earthly assumptions and growing closer to becoming your infinite, emotionally whole, authentic self. Even if you don't experience all the stages, you needn't worry that there's something wrong or that your awakening is incomplete. You may yet undergo further stages or sail through some of them without even noticing.

That which is unknown is becoming known; that which we forgot, we are remembering. Your soul knows and recalls countless truths, but you must go inward and coax this wisdom up through the levels of mind to utilize it on your human journey.

Your vision will become clear only when you can look into your own heart. Without, everything seems discordant; only within does it coalesce into unity. Who looks outside dreams; who looks inside awakes.

CARL JUNG

I describe the early stages of spiritual awakening as deconstruction stages because the architecture of the self seems to deconstruct. Then, as we move into the later reconstruction stages, we begin to rebuild our sense of self and reality anew.

The Shock Stage

The shock stage is the initial period that follows the triggering event that started your awakening. You've had a big surprise, and the whole context of your life is shifting. This can be the most demanding and accelerated phase when the most transformation happens in the least time.

Not so long ago, you took everyday things for granted, such as the solidity of reality, our societal paradigm, and your general aspirations and direction in life. At least you were reasonably sure that the world around you was as it appeared to be; you carried on as you always had, going with the general consensus, perhaps struggling emotionally with something, as we all tend to do. Life felt like a familiar and predictable construct.

Yet the potential for awakening may have been within you for years, like a telephone was ringing, and you had never answered it; when at last you did, the news you received had life-changing implications.

> *'I had an out-of-body experience that was so real I knew I wasn't dreaming. It felt like I left my body and was floating above myself. I could see the room around me and my body beneath. Then I heard my mother's voice as if she was in the room with me. How can that be? She passed away four years ago.'*

An out-of-body experience has far-reaching implications for how you perceive reality. If you can leave your body, then perhaps consciousness, or our essence, is not confined to physical form. You realize the implications of this, and countless other questions arise.

If you carry deeply held beliefs about life, such as, you *are* your physical body, and your consciousness is a product of the brain, when you then witness irrefutable evidence to the contrary, you're shocked into entertaining new ideas and beliefs.

> *'I never believed in extraterrestrial life and thought it the stuff of fiction. Then I watched a series of videos exposing evidence that extraterrestrials have been visiting Earth for thousands of years. I also learned that governments might be hiding this information and hundreds of artifacts from us. Why would they do that?'*

Sometimes these revelations can be hard to swallow. The *Cambridge Dictionary* defines cognitive dissonance as 'a state in which there is a difference between your experiences or behavior and your beliefs about what is true.'[3] Cognitive dissonance is responsible for much of the shock and denial you experience when new knowledge contradicts your existing beliefs. It is an unpleasant, unsettling feeling, where your ego refuses to release firmly held assumptions because life felt safe and secure as it was. Your ego was more or less a stable construct; it knew itself and how to function in the world. A contrasting, new belief means that life is different, and therefore uncertainty exists. Your ego dislikes uncertainty because it implies a lack of control.

When we feel we are losing control, we tend to perform actions that enable us to regain it and feel safer. The natural course of action, especially during awakening, is to begin searching and seeking for information, often frantically, to put the pieces of life back together. We attempt to restabilize and regain predictability, certainty, and control.

You might experience a range of unpleasant emotions during the shock stage, such as anxiety or confusion, mixed with positive emotions, such as jubilation and amazement because you're discovering profound knowledge that deeply resonates with you. There may be periods of blissful interconnectedness or mystical, magical days or weeks when you revel in your astonishing discoveries, and perhaps wonder, *Is this enlightenment?* Then shocking revelations, inner shadows, and challenges present themselves, and you enter darker moments once again.

Strong feelings are a great motivator to tell others about your realizations, and their responses might surprise you. Some show interest or even surprise, while others give you your first taste of 'awakening ridicule.'

Here are some tips to help you during the shock stage:

- Know that being shocked into awakening is normal and happens to many.

- Build and conserve your energies. Start to ditch processed foods and increase your consumption of life-giving fresh fruits, vegetables, and grains.

- Begin a meditation practice. When you feel the need for peace and calm, sit quietly and observe your breath for five minutes. When thoughts arise, allow them to gently float away and bring your attention back to your breath.

- If it's all too much, and if you want to, seek the company of others who share your new ideas, even if the only people you can find are online.

- If you have the urge to spend time alone, do so. You need time to process your perceptual shifts without judgment from others.

- You can use a crystal to help regulate your energies. I suggest black tourmaline or rose quartz. Visualize any negative energy within you flowing into the crystal through your hand. Wash the crystal at least twice per day during this time. Black tourmaline and rose quartz are calming protective crystals. Many other types are highly catalyzing and too powerful for this stage. They could unnecessarily accelerate your awakening. (Maybe don't meditate with amethyst on the top of your head just yet!)

Searching and Seeking

This is a common account of the searching and seeking stage of awakening, which is often extremely intense. Most who have gone through it will tell you that it's transformative and exhilarating, as well as lonely and strange. You spend much of your time trying to make sense of a world that becomes a lot weirder before becoming 'normal' again. Yet, your higher self seems to guide you by synchronistically placing relevant pieces of knowledge in front of you at the right time.

> *'Once it started, there was no stopping it. I was walking around in a daze, and my mind was swimming with information. I kept watching videos, reading books and articles so that I could make sense of things, but the more I learned, the more avenues there were to explore. One source of information synchronistically led to another.'*

During this stage, there is a clear challenge to the way you view life, yourself, and your purpose, and your ego cannot argue with the evidence. In response, you hunt for truths to stabilize your perceptions and help you feel safe in a newly uncertain world. For some, the truth is irresistible because consciousness cannot evolve without it, and the accompanying curiosity lures them down multiple deep rabbit holes on their way to finding it.

In the initial months of my awakening, I would stay up until 2 a.m. every morning, watching video after video, scouring books, even listening to channelings in the bath. Waking up to take the children to school was tough going, and although I was mindful of being a good mother throughout, I couldn't stop hunting for information, hungry for profound realizations.

Every time I had an epiphany, a warm 'phasing' sensation would sweep over my head, as if my brain was lighting up with excitement. I have now come to believe these were energetic shifts or upgrades in my consciousness, and that the sensation I was feeling was the distinctive gamma brainwave state. Brainwaves are patterns of electrical pulses that occur in our brain as millions of brain cells (neurons) communicate with each other using electricity. Beta brainwaves arise when we are active and busy, and alpha patterns emerge as we relax. Gamma brainwaves, on the other hand, are unusual because they sweep over our entire brain at once as if all neurons are firing in unison. Research has shown that Tibetan Buddhist monks produce an abundance of gamma waves during meditation practice. Gamma waves also arise when we practice in our field of expertise, meditate on love and compassion, have heightened focus, or meaningful realizations.

It helps to try to pace yourself during the searching and seeking stage. Numerous people experience burnout from information overload, feeling dizzy with realizations and exhausted by intense emotions. Remember there is plenty of time, no rush at all, and you are still just as safe and well as you have always been. An accelerated awakening experience is supposed to be impactful and profound to prompt us to mark it as a turning point in our lives and take notice, but we can still mindfully slow down.

> *'Researchers have discovered that when large groups of people meditate together, they influence the local population, and crime rates actually reduce. It's called the Maharishi effect, and it blew my mind! Why isn't this a commonly adopted practice across the world?'*

Although we are thrilled and delighted by much we learn, a sense of frustration can also set in as we wonder why everybody doesn't know about these critical concepts. The whole world could evolve and prosper if only things like the Maharishi effect were common knowledge.

You can also feel like you're going crazy, as your perceptions of life and reality shift further out of alignment from the people around you; you're frustrated they don't know this stuff and want to tell them! Loneliness can ensue, and more on that later. But for now, it's vital to realize that feeling 'crazy' is understandable during your awakening, but you can change your perspective. You are waking up from a 'crazy' world into a more discerning, insightful mode of being.

Taking a Balanced Path

We're especially open and receptive to all kinds of information during our intensive seeking stage, perhaps more so than ever in our lives. We are in a humble state of not knowing, so it's vital to choose our sources wisely or risk wandering into confusion and fear.

> *'I realized that my spirit guides are always with me, and I can communicate with them for guidance, especially if I'm going through a rough patch. But then I read in an online community that it's easy to be tricked by negative entities posing as spirit guides. Now I'm afraid that my house is full of evil spirits!'*

Realizations like this can cause our awakening to take a negative turn for a while. Our spiritual path can split and go either in a life-enhancing direction or a fearful one. The scenario described in the comment is a perfect illustration of someone not receiving the whole picture. Yes, it's possible to encounter beings of a negative nature, but there are certain conditions for this, methods of protection against it, and it's a relatively rare occurrence. During awakening, we are especially vulnerable to the onset of a low vibration, before we settle into our spiritual path, and incomplete snippets of information don't help. They even increase the likelihood of such circumstances happening. So, use your intuition and discernment when choosing your sources of information.

Your intuition is a fantastic compass for navigating the sea of information on spiritual, metaphysical, and paranormal topics. So if something doesn't resonate with you, take a new direction.

The Ego Goes to Town

Another intriguing and surprisingly common result of this stage is that the ego feels so privileged to be privy to such higher wisdom that an intense feeling of specialness arises, which in rare instances can even result in a messiah complex – a state in which a person believes they are a revered savior of humanity. It's merely a natural by-product of the early stages of awakening. For most, this belief passes as they realize that they're likely one of many working toward a better world. But if left unchecked, they can start assuming that they have all the knowledge they'll ever require and close themselves off to further learning and personal development. They move into a pseudo-enlightened state, where their egos take an unhealthy role. Following is a perfect example of this.

> 'I realize that we are all one energy. Oneness means that God is in everyone and everything, therefore I am God.'

Although I believe this statement to be true, it must be valid for everybody, not just one individual. If misconstrued, a person's ego can really go to town and begin to develop an unhealthy mind-set of self-importance and arrogance.

> *The more you know, the more you realize you don't know.*
>
> ARISTOTLE (ATTRIBUTED)

By accepting that the volume and flow of wisdom in the universe is endless and that your entire life is a journey of learning and experience, you can settle into an enjoyably paced exploration of subject matter to fill your heart and mind steadily. No one has all the answers, and we're all in this reality together.

Grounding Yourself While You're Thirsting for Knowledge

Information often arrives in waves, so your emotions can go up and down as realizations sweep through your consciousness. As with every stage of awakening, if this happens, it's likely supposed to. But if you're excessively stressed and in a dark place, take steps to find peace and balance.

🦋 EXERCISE: WALKING MINDFULNESS 🦋

Perform a walking mindfulness meditation to give yourself a respite. This process helps you find peace and calm your thoughts, offering an opportunity for your subconscious mind to integrate what you've learned.

1. Take a walk, preferably in nature. A park is great as long as there are some trees and greenery. If you can, go barefoot so that you are grounded.

2. As you begin walking, settle into comfortable rhythmic breaths, preferably into your belly.

3. Bring your awareness to the present moment and arrive in your body and mind.

4. When thoughts come to you, gently and nonjudgmentally allow them to float away into the sky, watching them go with your mind's eye, and bring your attention back to you and your surroundings.

5. Focus on your breath for a few minutes. How does it feel as you inhale and exhale? How does it sound?

6. Now, spend a few minutes observing your steps. How does it feel to take each step?

7. Next, be mindful of your surroundings. What do you see? Mentally describe the sights to yourself. What do you hear, feel, or smell?

8. Lastly, intuitively connect with the natural energies around you. Sit under a tree if possible, and mentally reach out to other beings around you like plants, bushes, flowers, trees, and animals. Imagine what it is like to be them. Do this for as long as you wish.

The Ego Dissolves

The next stage is when, potentially, your ego breaks down, and you begin to discover your authentic self. This process is responsible for much of the fear and anxiety felt during awakening, it overlaps significantly with other stages, and not everyone experiences it fully.

The ego is defined in various ways by different people, but generally, it embodies everything that makes up who you believe you are or should be in a human lifetime. It is the tangled web of you, the illusions and constructs of the mind that form the concept of a person going by a name. The ego can include:

◉ your beliefs and perceptions about yourself, your self-image (for example: I am attractive, or I am respectable.)

◉ your perceived identity (for example: I am a nurse, or I am a father.)

◉ your beliefs and values about who or what you should be (for example: I should be successful, or I should be environmentally conscious.)

◉ your social persona (how you present yourself in different situations)

◉ the personality characteristics you aspire to maintain (such as being kind or diligent)

◉ your perceptions of your roles in life (for example: I provide care, or I lead the team.)

- your assumptions about how others perceive you and how you want to be perceived

- the story of your life

All these contribute to your:

- opinions, attitudes, and behaviors

- wants, needs, desires, and aspirations

- emotions

There are infinite combinations of factors that make every person unique. It's important to remember that you are not your ego; it is a construct. You are a pure point of infinite awareness that observes the world without judgment before any aspects of ego come in to play and color what you sense, perceive, feel, say, or do. You are in the process of seeking and realizing your pure awareness during awakening.

Our ego comes about with little or no conscious thought or decision-making; it arises due to assumptions and beliefs we have collected over time. Think about it: Did you decide every little thing about yourself? Do you plan how to behave when meeting friends? Whether you do or you don't, you still likely present a persona. Do you choose how to feel every time you look in the mirror? Maybe your opinions of how you look and how you should look don't always match. Did you mindfully appoint your priorities in life, or did they simply arise? Perhaps you have assumed what should be important to you. Did you decide to adopt the values and norms of your culture, or did they naturally become part of you?

The ego always wants more. More attachments, identifications, achievements, distractions, recognition – more stuff, you name it, the ego wants it. It's a tiring treadmill to be on, and you might *still* come up feeling empty and, therefore, need even more. But where is our true infinite beingness in all this? Where is lasting contentment?

Former Self to New Self

When we undergo a spiritual awakening, we question a lifetime of assumptions and beliefs, often for the first time and urgently; therefore, our life's context makes an incredible shift. Because assumed constructs make up the fabric of the ego itself, once we begin to release them, the ego (the illusory part of us) starts to dissolve. And it doesn't like it; hence, we often end up experiencing fear, anxiety, confusion, and other tumultuous emotions. As we attempt to rebuild and regain stability, we begin to ask questions like the following.

- Who am I?

- Have I been living a lie?

- Are my pastimes worthwhile?

- Is my job meaningful?

- Whom can I trust?

- How valid are my priorities?

- Am I safe?

- What is my purpose?

- ◉ What is the meaning of life?

- ◉ What is the nature of reality?

- ◉ Is there a God, and what is he, she, or it?

It's best to ask these questions from the perspective of our infinite self, using our intuition to evaluate the answers, rather than from the standpoint of our ego, which isn't usually so informed, because it's a human construct. The ego part of you doesn't want to die, of course, so it hangs on for dear life. Once you begin exploring your true self, however, this higher part of you increasingly takes the lead, and what's left of your ego generally settles down.

> '*I realize that I have been prioritizing work so much that I have neglected my family. I thought that money and success would provide happiness for my partner and kids, when actually all they want is to be with me. I guess I assumed that once I had climbed the career ladder, I would allow myself time to enjoy life. But time flew by, the children are teenagers, and I've been working all the time. If only I realized I could stop and have fun with them at any time, and that happiness was possible in any now moment all along.*'

This kind of realization has the power to transform the self. Our busy ego often causes us to miss the present moment. Identifying with our career and success can be meaningful, yes, but we should strike a balance between all aspects of life. To feel complete, our infinite true self doesn't *need* rewards defined by society. Our ego, however, doesn't know any better. Built on earthly assumptions, it thinks these things are of the utmost importance.

We struggle to find fulfillment using society's benchmarks while performing the same old actions to achieve it. Maybe the answer is a simpler one, found within us *and* distinguished from society. The genuine you is not another copy of what the general public thinks a person should be. The ego naturally adopts the norms and behaviors of society because it desires to fit in, to be validated and accepted by others. Some religions and social structures don't want you to change or break away to find your own path because doing so reduces the strength and validity of the group. Society wants you to conform to the status quo for its very survival. But if you are going to find your individuality – while remaining mindful you are one with all – it's necessary to observe from your soul's point of view. Why would you want to find your true self? There's likely more fulfillment in truly knowing, loving, and expressing your authentic, infinite, soul-reflecting self than in continuing on with an involuntarily created ego, right?

A Little Bit of Ego

Now, let's remember one little thing: You do need a certain level of ego to function in society. Just by dressing smartly for work, being interested in gardening, or saying 'I love cats,' you exhibit traits of your ego, and these are normal, everyday things. The difference is, however, that during your awakening and beyond, you can reconstruct as you see fit the amount of ego you need. You can intuitively and consciously choose who you want to be, what to wear, what to read, your actions, attitudes, aims, beliefs, and more, without blindly conforming to trends, social norms, and the general consensus – all the while being mindful that you are actually an infinite point of awareness experiencing a human existence. You can redesign your life intuitively.

Who Is Your True Self?

It's useful to note that during ego deconstruction, there is often a pressing urge to rebuild yourself, your life, and purpose quickly to regain stability. During this time, be aware of your ego trying to grab new identities in a hurry, because it hates the uncertainty of the whole awakening process. It's vital to take your time to consider who you really are at the deepest levels. As you go, though, try to accept all aspects of yourself no matter what, even the parts you might wish to change, because self-acceptance leads to self-love. Instead of resisting your ego, you can work with it to heal it.

Ego dissolution can be a real gift! When do you ever get to start all over again and explore the most authentic you? Allow your higher self to guide you because it knows your distinctive potential. It is your true self, after all, far in the future, further evolved, and in another dimension. You can get your ego out of the driver's seat, make it a helpful passenger, and be guided by your higher awareness instead. Before you start, ask yourself: What aspects of myself contribute to my spiritual evolution and which are standing in the way?

❧ Exercise: Map of Self ❧

Make an intuitive map of your true, authentic self. Do this by connecting with your higher self through intuition, allowing your inner knowing to guide you. You can clarify muddled thoughts, feel for your truth, and lay realizations out methodically. Often, as we step into new characteristics and aspirations, unhelpful ones naturally fall away. You'll need a pen and paper for this exercise.

1. Relax and begin to allow your intuition to flow. It's that feeling that guides you with authenticity in exciting directions. Try *feeling* for your excitement and joy rather than *deciding*.

2. Take all the traits you admire and appreciate most about yourself and write them in one column; for example, kind, helpful, fun, sociable, creative, intuitive, a healer, a lover of writing.

3. Beneath this, in the same column, list any aims that fill you with enthusiasm; for example, to increase motivation, be more focused, increase self-love, start a business.

4. Beside each of these traits and aims write a description of how you can nurture or achieve them, starting with: 'I can' as you affirm to yourself that these things are achievable. Here are some examples.

   ~ Creative – I can nurture my creativity by putting time aside to write a blog.

   ~ A healer – I can attend a local acupressure training course.

~ Increase self-love – I can work on releasing the past and accepting everything about myself on my journey to becoming my true self.

~ Start a business – Once I have completed my acupressure course, I can perform healing in my spare time outside of work until I build up a client base.

There you have it, a heart-led, intuitively created plan for your path toward your most wonderful self. Feel free to amend and enhance your map of self as you experience further growth and realizations. Any time you feel you're losing sight of the bigger picture, come back and reaffirm where you're heading.

Loneliness

This stage is also known as the hermit phase. We can end up rather isolated during awakening whether we like it or not. Some people gladly welcome their solitude during this stage; it all depends on your natural coping strategies and the extent to which you require the comfort and inclusion of others. Isolation – and loneliness for some – usually creeps in after the shock stage, while the searching-and-seeking and ego-dissolving stages are still in full swing.

If you don't know who you are anymore, interacting with others can be hugely challenging. Those desiring to be alone do so because they can't endure pressure from others during this time. They disconnect from the outside world, with all its responsibilities and expectations, feeling very sensitive and vulnerable. Psychic abilities may be surfacing, energies moving, and a process of life reevaluation happening, so it's a time to go within. Excessive external stimuli only intensify this sensitive process. Often, though, we still need to go to work to pay the bills, so we drag ourselves out, dreading facing others who are still ever so deeply entrenched in the earthly attitudes and beliefs we're shaking off. We continue healing, purging, and discovering while trying to hold it together in normal daily life.

> 'How can I face everyone at work when all I want to do is be at home alone? I'm still trying to make sense of things. I literally don't know who I am anymore, or whether my job is worth doing, and all my workmates talk about is football, hyped-up news stories, and what they did last time they went out drinking. Usually, I enjoy all that, but it doesn't appeal to me anymore. I'm going through a lot mentally and physically, and I just can't pretend that everything is okay.'

As your priorities and perceptions shift further out of alignment from those of your friends, colleagues, and family, you can feel very lonely even in their presence. How can they understand what you're going through if they have no concept of awakening? Things that mattered to you before, what you identified with, your goals are all changing, and you have yet to meet anyone on your new wavelength – you might not be ready to either. We'll go deeper into relating to loved ones, workmates, and reintegrating with society soon.

Many also have pronounced mood swings during the loneliness stage, and because they don't want to show others this temporary yet volatile version of themselves, they isolate. Interruptions are frustrating and responsibilities draining. Some individuals, however, want to be around others because they feel excessively anxious and require comfort and reassurance.

As you awaken to more and more concepts, it feels like you're in a small boat drifting away from the shore where your friends and loved ones are standing. As the tide takes you farther away, you realize they can no longer hear you. It seems as though you are disappearing from sight. Family and friends often worry about you and begin to pass judgment on the material you are reading and watching, and this makes you want to withdraw. It feels like no one gets you during a time when you need understanding and support the most. If you're lucky, you'll know someone on the spiritual path who can validate your experiences and tell you about their own. What an incredible relief! They may offer support and recommend practices that helped them.

Accepting How You Feel

The early stages of awakening can be alarming. We're exposed, still aimless, and in a state of self-preservation. You can't expect to carry on as usual when the person you were is gone and the new you has yet to take shape. Your confidence is likely low, you don't know how or who to be, and you need time to rebuild, without judgment or interference from others. Many begin to feel benevolently guided as the quiet of loneliness allows them to receive guidance from ancestral spirits, spirit guides, and higher aspects of themselves. Whether you want to be alone or not, it's likely vital for your transformation. After all, it is you that must deconstruct, rebuild, heal, and discover. No one can do it for you. Once you're ready, you can go out and walk your path.

My husband – before I met him – quit his job and isolated himself during his awakening. Although not the best idea financially, he had no choice. He had only the urge to go within and meditate, basically full time, which served to intensify his awakening, leading him into a dark night of the soul and back.

What can you do if you are going through the loneliness stage?

- Know that loneliness is a side effect of your awakening, and things will improve.

- Give yourself time to heal. The initial realizations have come thick and fast, and your consciousness needs time to integrate them.

- You might be lonely at this time to make you stronger. We all need companionship to help us feel validated, included, and loved, but know that in being alone right now, you are practicing being independent, whole, and complete as an individual. If you can get through this, then you can get through anything.

- If you're sinking too low, at least talk to your loved ones about how you feel. Consider letting them know that you're going through an emotional crisis and that you need support. They'll surely understand that request – even if not *what* you are going through – and they *can* be emotionally present. Also, remember there are spiritual guides and healers out there, and booking a session and chatting with one of them may help you along. There are also online groups where you can interact with others who are going through the same process.

⊚ Trust in your wonderful qualities. There's no need to be alone in the future. People will still love to be around you, and if not, consider that they don't deserve you.

⊚ Have faith that relationships and friendships will be even better than before. Now that you're developing a new heartfelt interest, you'll be able to share it with other likeminded people when you're ready.

⊚ Remember you're never alone, because your spirit guides are always with you. If you relax for a while and set the intention to connect with them, you can sense their love.

The Purging and the Dark Night of the Soul

Any unhealed pain, betrayal, neglect, frustrations, resentments, unhelpful programming, or anything else that requires healing, are all stored in your subconscious mind, and now it's purging time. Not everyone experiences the dark night of the soul, but many do experience the purging of negative energies. The purging tends to happen first.

Purging an Accumulation of Energies

You might have been experiencing sadness or anxiety before your awakening, but now, even more negative energies are surfacing. It's like many hands reaching up from deep within your psyche and slapping you around the face, one by one. Why does this happen? Seeing as you're in the process of shifting toward a higher vibration, lower vibrations are releasing from your consciousness. Your shadow side consists of aspects of self that follow you around like an actual shadow, escaping your awareness. But during the purging stage, they become apparent, often a little too apparent.

We purge the negative energies we've accumulated during our lifetime – the excess of them anyway – so that our consciousness can leap in vibration. Otherwise, unhelpful perceptions, assumptions, and beliefs can corrupt and discolor our discoveries moving forward. We may take a slightly negative path, one where we unknowingly use our newfound wisdom in destructive ways, perhaps negatively influencing others or ourselves. For some, there's not much to purge, but for others, there's plenty, especially if they've had a difficult life. More opportunities for healing and purging present themselves later, over time; however, this early stage of purging is often the most intense. Like a shaken can of beer, the contents burst out under pressure the moment you open it up.

Purging symptoms can include:

⊚   mood swings

⊚   memories surfacing

⊚   shaking, twitching, and vibration

⊚   profound inner realizations

⊚   involuntary movements

- nausea

- rashes

- headaches

- dizziness

- sweating

- sleeplessness

As your heart chakra opens (due to realizing the truth of love and understanding) and your third eye opens (due to your consciousness expanding), you'll become increasingly sensitive to ambient energies, the energies of others, and the collective consciousness, exacerbating purging. It is cyclically stimulated; the more you open up, the more you purge, the more you purge, the more you open up.

The mind and body are *one*; therefore, signs of past trauma are often present in the body as pain or discomfort. As darker energy moves and releases, it sometimes does so with difficulty, causing more discomfort. The following exercise is one way to ease this process.

🦋 EXERCISE: CLEARING BODY SHADOWS 🦋

This process involves visualization. Some people are unable to hold mental images, and this is called aphantasia. If this is the case for you, then use your sense of 'just knowing' or feel into what is happening.

1. Put on some meditation music and relax or meditate for 20 minutes.

2. With your eyes closed, sense or picture your body within your mind.

3. Allow your sense of knowing (claircognizance) to come through or use your mind's eye (clairvoyance) to detect any 'body shadows.' These are any areas of dark or negative energy within your body, including your head.

4. Focus on one shadow, allow it to communicate with you, and listen and observe.

5. What follows, if you are willing and open, will be a flood of knowing or mental images, usually memories, of unhealed events or circumstances from the past.

6. Accept these and try to gain an understanding of why they have come to mind. Search your feelings.

7. Understanding leads to forgiveness, so find ways to forgive others whom you observe in your thoughts and memories, and remember to have forgiveness for yourself, too, if necessary.

8. Wish the body shadows love and healing.

9. Will the shadow-energy to clear from your body. Sense or visualize it flowing out and away into Creation.

10. Open your eyes when you're ready, and do things of a relaxing, light nature for the following few days.

The Dark Night Arrives

Stay with me. This book will definitely take a happier turn soon. But let's move on to the dark night of the soul. Not everyone has it or needs it. It can follow the purging, or it can happen later, perhaps after being on the spiritual path for years. It arrives for many reasons, possibly due to realizations about the past or disillusionment with the world. The dark night is a deep spiritual crisis where we plunge into the dark depths of our psyche while on our journey toward the light. It can feel more like a fight to survive rather than part of a journey toward enlightenment. You go into another world, and the challenge is to come back, bringing your gifts with you.

> The dark night of the soul comes just before revelation.
> When everything is lost, and all seems darkness,
> then comes the new life and all that is needed.
> JOSEPH CAMPBELL

Before we can reach new heights, we must sometimes sink very low and genuinely understand what it is like to be in the abyss. It often presents itself as the reliving of desperate times, emotional turmoil, the complete loss of self, and total separation from everything worldly. We are deep within our inner world.

Am I Seeing Things?

The darkness inside often manifests before our eyes in the form of malevolent spirits, interdimensional beings, demons, portals, and thought-form manifestations. Our energies can also become so focused that we might inadvertently move objects with our mind, cause electrical appliances to malfunction, and lightbulbs to break. We might sense we have been touched or pushed by mischievous spirits, hear them thumping around, or even think we are possessed. There are a couple of reasons for these phenomena, and some people end up fearing dark energies and spirits due to this, but this is not necessary. We create our reality via thought, and if we focus enough energy toward something we *believe* is there, it can actually develop a level of consciousness of its own. I'm not saying that spirits are imaginary, but we *make* many of them real. Another possibility is that they *are* there, but this is actually much rarer than thought-form creation.

When we exude intense negative energy, we become delightfully attractive to dark spirits, and we might attract one that hangs around for a while. But we can perform inner work, meditation, and other techniques to raise our overall vibration so that we become horribly high vibrational to pesky spirits. Your energy is unpalatable if your vibration is rising. Of course, even after the dark night of the soul has passed, we all have days when we feel sad and down, but that doesn't mean spirits will return, far from it. They'll observe your heart-centered attitude and positive aims and want nothing to do with you. Also, remember that if you believe you are vulnerable, you will create vulnerability; but during the dark night, we can't help but feel vulnerable. So the following can help, as can methods of protection and raising your vibration, which are discussed in Chapters 6 and 8.

🦋 Exercise: Cleansing Your Energies 🦋 with Smoke

You can clear unpleasant energies from your surroundings and yourself.

~ Cleanse using responsibly sourced sage, sandalwood, rose, or frankincense incense.

~ Carefully and slowly, waft the smoke around your body, from head to toe, for two minutes.

~ As you do so, repeat the affirmation, 'I am fully protected in the light of love.'

~ Waft the smoke around your home with care, paying attention to corners, high and low places, cupboards, and other nooks and crannies.

~ Repeat this affirmation as you go, 'All unwanted energies or beings leave now, and be replaced with light. This place is sacred.'

Thought-forms should evaporate, and if you have collected one or two beings of a negative nature, they'll naturally drift away. If not, you can contact a spiritual medium specializing in spirit release; they are often very effective. Remember that this dimension of Earth is *your* reality, not the spirits'. You are far more powerful than any such being. They only harm you by scaring you, so don't let them.

Awakening or Psychosis?

Spiritual awakening or emergency can sometimes be mistaken for psychosis. Many are given pharmaceuticals, which can dull the process, or are committed to mental health institutions. If you are receiving medication, it's always best to continue it during the darker stages of awakening, lest you risk exacerbating the situation. Yes, the process must run its course and might be less profound while you're on medication, but you don't want to put yourself at risk. It would be beneficial to society if spiritual crises were recognized and given credence more often, as most health professionals don't believe in such phenomena, leaving experiencers feeling alone and misunderstood.

> *'I sweated and shook as I lay on the couch and felt like I was dying. There was a presence in the room with me. Suddenly, I felt a pain in my stomach, and a shadowy being rose out of my body and stood over me. It was like a dark version of myself standing and staring at me. There were moments when I could see through its eyes, observing myself. I shouted 'What do you want?' and a second later I felt intense guilt about things I had done. I often feel a little like that, but it was incredibly strong that time. I knew that if I were to get through it, I'd need to forgive myself. So I closed my eyes, and that's what I did. Then I told the shadowy figure it could go, but as I looked up, it had already gone.'*

The National Health Service's website defines *psychosis* as, 'when people lose some contact with reality. This might involve seeing or hearing things that other people cannot see or hear (hallucinations) and believing things that are not actually true (delusions).[4] You can see the similarities between this definition and spiritual emergency. Those going through awakening undoubtedly interpret the world differently from those around them, even if they are not going through the dark night. They might speak of spiritual experiences that health professionals may consider delusional. But if we are going through awakening, it doesn't necessarily mean we are mentally unwell. Many hallucinations and delusions happen for healing purposes as we release bottled-up, negative energy, liberating us from negative emotion. For many, it's part of the process.

Societal consensus decrees that if the paranormal cannot be measured and proven, then it must not exist, and that those who experience such events are ill. Of course, real psychosis arises in individuals, but we mustn't overlook the spiritual. What if the dark night of the soul, although unpleasant, is very beneficial for us overall? I know I emerged from it feeling reborn. For many of us, it is a mystical and meaningful experience showing us the unknown, and if we pay attention fully, we can come to terms with our shadows and heal them.

Those Pesky Helicopters

I had terrible trouble with helicopters during my dark night journey. For some reason, they were flying over my house several times a week. I could see their lights in the dark, and they hovered directly overhead for several minutes at a time, loudly and clearly. Perhaps they were searching for someone, maybe it was an army exercise, or perhaps they were a figment of my imagination. Who knows? I lived with my kids, but it always happened after they were asleep, so I could never gain proof. I did mention it to a neighbor, and he simply confirmed that helicopters sometimes flew over but didn't acknowledge their excessive presence. The trouble was, I thought they were monitoring me because I knew things I shouldn't know. So I became exceedingly paranoid that they'd harm my family, and I would lie awake all night even after they'd gone. I never had run-ins with helicopters before or since and was probably manifesting them, bringing them into my reality because the more I feared them, the more the deep humming, whirring sound arrived and persisted.

In addition to the purging symptoms, the dark night of the soul can induce:

- anxiety, sadness, and other unpleasant emotions
- waking up in the night (often at 3 a.m. for some reason)
- depression
- paranoia
- auditory and visual hallucinations
- astral travel
- flashbacks of your current or previous lifetimes
- vivid dreams and nightmares
- sleepwalking
- exhaustion

- fever

- psychic sensitivity (opening of the psychic senses)

- manifesting unfavorable events

- thought-form creation

Remain open to contacting your health-care professional if you are concerned, if the problems persist, or if they occur outside the context of awakening.

Other Triggers of the Dark Night

Sometimes we uncover gloomy information that makes us feel like the end of the world is imminent. We might fear war, disaster, or totalitarianism like in George Orwell's book *1984*. Whether these circumstances arise or not, essential preparations begin to occupy our thoughts. I bought an SAS survival handbook and planned which area of the countryside to take camping stuff in case of some catastrophe. This illustrates where thoughts can go during the dark night of the soul. The preoccupation with death and risk is symptomatic of our ego experiencing death, so it brings up thoughts of doom and danger coming from every direction. It actually helps to prepare for such circumstances – to a reasonable extent – if we fear them, because in feeling prepared, we alleviate worry. I felt better once I bought my handbook, but it has sat on a shelf ever since.

A common phenomenon during the dark night of the soul is psychically perceiving disturbances in the collective consciousness.

> *'I feel constant anxiety and anger about what goes on in the world. I had to stop myself from watching the news because it feels biased and like a never-ending source of fear. I feel other people's struggles so deeply.'*

We also suspect that humanity's evolution is being held back, and feel frustrated and powerless to do anything about it. I always say that you can't fix the world on your own, but you can do your part, and if everyone did their part, then the world would change. So you can set an example. If you proceed with this renewed purpose, you can begin to move more quickly through the dark night of the soul where this type of frustration is the cause.

Working through It

The dark night does pass over time and varies in length from person to person, although for some it can hang on for a long time. So how can you traverse it more easily? You can try the following:

⊚ Accept your feelings. This requires a certain amount of bravery, but you are feeling this way for a reason. You are becoming aware of, and coming to terms with, your shadows.

⊚ Become the observer of scary phenomena if they are happening and transcend them. Instead of being a participant, watch nonjudgmentally as visions, visitations, and purging play out. But seek emotional support if you are sinking too low.

⊚ Consider that there is no imminent danger and that you are safe and well.

⊚ Employ psychic protection and remember your power. Protection methods are covered in Chapter 6, but remember here that your attitude, feelings, and beliefs create your reality to a great extent. If you believe you are powerless, then powerlessness is what you'll create. It can be hard to step into your power at the moment but entertain the possibility of doing so.

⊚ Commence a routine ritual, such as the exercise on cleansing your energies with smoke (*see p.86*), or daily meditation practice surrounded by your favorite crystals. You'll feel like you are doing something useful and constructive to help yourself.

~

Chapter 4

Reconstruction Stages of Awakening

After the deconstruction stages, we begin to reconstruct. You've changed, and your life is like a canvas ready for colorful paint. Allow yourself to be the artist. You've learned a great deal, and if your vibration sank low, it's probably rising once more. It's time to use your newfound wisdom to shape your unique path and self. What an exciting time to explore new possibilities! Rarely is this journey easy, so don't be hard on yourself if it's not. However, positivity and excitement are more likely to find you from this point forward.

Noticing More Phenomena

You may have already witnessed or experienced extraordinary phenomena even before your awakening, but as you begin to open your heart and mind, profound experiences occur more frequently. Why is this? Because we are more receptive to the unusual, we're *allowing* miracles to happen. It's not wishful thinking; these are authentic experiences that occur when you least expect them and, often, when you need them most. Before awakening, while under earthly illusions, you likely had no thought for sacred signs, synchronicities, or mystical experiences, and perhaps didn't believe in psychic senses or our energetic form. Therefore, many of these phenomena were blocked from your reality.

If our higher self means for us to live part of our lifetime under earthly illusions, it would rather spoil it were we to see 1111 every day. This would trigger our awakening before it's supposed to happen. So once it *is* time to awaken, and we freely choose to open up to such experiences, they enter our frame of reference. The human experience is one of illusion and assumptions, and Creation likes it that way in order to observe if we'll transcend it. But upon awakening, we depart, for the most part, from the human illusion, and in this state of surrender, Creation can show us what we weren't ready or willing to observe before.

I Think I Might Be Psychic

We start to notice our psychic and empathic abilities, or at least accidental occurrences of them. We pick up on the thoughts and feelings of others and experience them as our own. The HeartMath Institute researches the magnetic fields produced by the heart and their potential for energetic communication. *'The results of these experiments have led us to conclude that the nervous system acts as an antenna, which is tuned to and responds to the magnetic fields produced by the hearts of other individuals.'*[5]

The electromagnetic field of the heart can be detected up to three feet away. Does this mean that when one person's energy field intersects with another's there's potential for the sharing of feelings? The HeartMath Institute notes, *'We have proposed that these same rhythmic patterns also can transmit emotional information via the electromagnetic field into the environment, which can be detected by others and processed in the same manner as internally generated signals.'*[6]

Usually, we believe we experience only our own thoughts and feelings, but it's likely we also share them with others. It's not like taking thoughts out of someone's mind like files out of a computer but more like file sharing.

> *'I collected my child from school and asked her what she did that day. Before she could answer, an image popped into my mind of a giraffe with bits of pasta stuck to it. I also felt a chilly cold-water sensation. She then said that she had made a picture of a giraffe and, although it was fun, it didn't turn out well because she knocked over the cup for rinsing brushes, and it made a mess. I was pretty stunned, and after reassuring her, I asked what she used for the picture. She said that she had stuck stars and pieces of dry pasta to it.'*

Accidental psychic occurrences, although surprising, help you see proof of your emerging abilities. What are the chances of guessing all those details? Psychic visions and intuitive knowing happen to many people, but even after awakening, we tend to forget about them or brush them off as coincidences. If you wrote them all down and your synchronicities, too, over time you'd have a log of a pretty magical life.

> *All the powers in the universe are already ours. It is we who have put our hands before our eyes and cry that it is dark.*
>
> SWAMI VIVEKANANDA

We all have psychic abilities, but rarely practice using them, and we're told they're not even a thing, so we're not very good at them. Universal powers are already ours, and while we lament the suffering in the world, we fail to observe the abilities within us that could unite us all – not just for psychic readings or predictions, but to connect us in ways that we can only imagine, perhaps in the sharing of all wisdom, truth, and knowing, mind to mind, accessible to anyone, anytime. No longer would darkness be hidden. If someone were suffering, we'd know it and be there to help. If someone were planning terrible acts, they'd receive instant psychic healing from all over the globe.

Anyway, I often get carried away about ways to change the world, and perhaps you do too. It is another surefire symptom of awakening, and one that doesn't tend to stop.

Here's an example of how our psychic abilities spontaneously emerge.

> *'I was out shopping and thought of my friend and his partner, neither of whom I had seen in six months. About ten minutes later, I bumped into them in the car park. I told them I was just thinking of them!'*

How often has this kind of thing happened to you? We often immediately forget the 'coincidence,' but if you think about it, it's probably happened many times throughout your life. You look at your phone right before a loved one calls or messages, or you wonder where that package is you ordered and then it turns up at the door, or you know what someone is going to say before they say it. During and after awakening, precognition happens more frequently because we are beginning to believe. It merely feels like having a thought or a feeling. Psychic skills are very subtle, and in having these experiences, you are using your innate, natural gifts. It's lovely to receive evidence of the spiritual and metaphysical nature of your own consciousness, proof that you're more than the human being you see in the mirror.

During this time, you might have the urge to pick up some tarot cards, the I Ching, rune stones, or a pendulum, or to learn channeling or mediumship. Your inner wisdom wants to surface, and perhaps a higher aspect of yourself is knocking on the doors of your mind, ready to communicate.

What a Synchronous Day!

Have you ever had days where number patterns seem to find you everywhere? Perhaps just when you needed comfort, the time on your phone showed 2222. It's a corker when the date is the 22nd, and your battery life shows 22 per cent too. Carl Jung described synchronicity as 'A meaningful coincidence of two or more events, where something other than the probability of chance is involved.'[7]

Something happens that seems beyond chance, and we begin to wonder if reality, or perhaps our guides or higher self, are trying to communicate with us. Awakening can multiply and intensify synchronistic experiences, but instead of dismissing them, we explore their meaning. What was I thinking at the time? What was I feeling? What was the context? We can also use our intuition, another psychic sense in accelerated development, to feel for the meaning and direction behind the message.

> *'I was standing on the platform at the train station, waiting for the train after work. The sun was shining, and its warmth was comforting. My awakening had begun more than six months before, and I was still feeling aimless, like a wanderer in a strange land. Just then, the sun seemed to touch my soul, and I had a thought that pierced through my mind like a blade. I realized that what you seek is seeking you. Just then, a large, bright-blue butterfly began to flutter around me. It was so beautiful that I got my phone out and began to film it. As I did so, it landed at the center of my chest and stayed there. It was like a mystical confirmation of my thought, that as I was seeking to film this beautiful creature, it sought to find rest on me.'*

We can interpret synchronicities as confirmation of our thoughts and feelings, as reassurance when we are feeling down, or as divine inspiration and direction. Number synchronicities are important to many people, and although the combinations have standard meanings, what they mean to you is more relevant. I urge you to observe all forms of synchronicity. Information can synchronistically land in your lap at just the right time, especially during awakening. Your higher self likely has a plan for you to awaken to the most useful wisdom and knowledge that you need at that moment, which will open your mind just enough for the next realization. You're learning things in an optimal order to prevent confusion. Events, too, can align synchronistically as your higher self guides you along your optimal path. For example, meeting the love of your life by chance, when neither of you intended to go to an event but unusual circumstances led to you both attending. Concepts, words, sentences, and symbols might also appear in your reality, in many places and at numerous times throughout the day. Ask yourself, What is the synchronicity trying to tell me?

My husband, Antti, frequently experiences incredible synchronicity to do with herons. We chatted online for a few weeks before we first met in person, and during this time, I saw a magnificent heron by a lake in the forest. Antti had never mentioned a word to me about herons up until this point, but I felt the urge to send him a picture of it. Very surprised, he messaged back to say that the heron is his spirit animal. He must have thought it a good sign for our upcoming date! So, our first date came around, and we were on a train, heading to a restaurant. He was emphasizing to me the extent to which he encounters herons, such as in pictures, articles, people mentioning them, and seeing them in real life. At that moment, as if to provide ultimate proof, a large gray heron swooped out of nowhere and flew parallel with the train. It seemed to be looking right at us. Erupting with laughter, I assured him that I definitely believed him.

*❝ This is called synchronicity – a state
in which you almost feel as if you are in
a collaborative arrangement with fate. ❞*

WAYNE DYER

I find that by observing and listening to synchronicity, I continue heading in the best direction in life. Synchronicity is like a trail of breadcrumbs, showing you your most advantageous way forward. The future is not written because it changes with every decision we make, but I believe that we decide aspects of our optimal life path before birth. Synchronicity keeps us on this path, if we are observing, of course, and awakening helps us to realize that it's in our best interests to observe.

Abilities Surfacing

Your inner and outer worlds are communicating now more than ever, and further phenomena that might intensify due to awakening are:

- clairvoyance, claircognizance, clairaudience, and clairsentience (*see Chapter 6*).

- spirit communication

- past-life remembering

- visions

- precognition

- empathic sense

- seeing energies and interdimensional beings (such as elementals and nature spirits)

- sensing the energies of objects and places

- psychic connection with nature

- telepathy (two-way mind-to-mind communication)

- seeing auras

- lucid dreaming

- 'downloads' (wisdom and knowing being dumped into your mind all at once, from higher aspects of self)

🦋 EXERCISE: JOURNALING SYNCHRONICITIES 🦋 AND ABILITIES

Chart your synchronicities to see where they lead, and log your psychic and other spiritual experiences to gain clarity. You may wish to develop one of your abilities as a specialized practice, and this will assist in identifying your strengths and marked abilities.

~ Approach this long-term process with the aim of gaining understanding.

~ Use a diary with dates and plenty of space to write. You can refer back to it when phenomena occur.

~ Preferably, carry the diary with you, because synchronicities and accidental psychic occurrences can happen when you are out, and you might forget to write them down.

~ Note each phenomenon, what happened, your mood and thoughts at the time, and anything else significant.

~ Note any type of phenomenon I've mentioned in this book, even the most seemingly insignificant. They may become meaningful later.

~ Use the back pages of the diary to tally similar events and note patterns of experiences.

~ Relax for about 20 minutes, and observe the significant patterns. Ask yourself questions, using your intuition to find the answers.

~ For synchronicities: What are they saying? What do they mean to me? What do I learn from them? How did they make me feel?

~ For psychic abilities: What ability is emerging as a strength? How do I feel about it? What does it mean in my life? What do I learn from it?

~ Ask yourself any other questions you feel appropriate and do the same for any other kinds of phenomena you experience.

~ Write your answers down, too, so that you can refer back to them later.

~ As patterns of significance form, and your intuition helps you with the meanings, you will gain more clarity on your spiritual journey.

Making Life Changes

Life surely does change when we move through awakening. As we transition from the deconstruction stages into reconstruction, our wants, needs, desires, values, beliefs, behaviors, and other aspects of self get a reworking. Not everyone's life will drastically transform, but for some, it does. If material and societal ideals defined you as a person, then your life might change a great deal. If, for example, you always felt a deep connection with nature, loved to help others, and suspected that life goes on after death, then you might not experience such drastic changes. Adjustments don't always happen all at once, but this stage of awakening might be the most significant period of change in your life.

I laughed when I categorized the types of life changes that occur, because all nine of them begin with the letter *p*, and they are:

- priorities

- preferences

- perceptions

- personality

- pastimes

- practices

- people

- profession

- purpose

Priorities

Why do our priorities change? Well, if your beliefs change, then what you think is significant also changes, so you bump up the importance level of certain things. If you no longer believe in our societal structure, you might decide on new ways of living, perhaps self-sustainably. If you no longer believe in climbing hierarchies, then your independence might increase. Should you begin to think you are infinite energetic consciousness, you might choose to live a simpler, freer, intuitively led life.

The trouble is, sometimes we can't just make sweeping changes, owing to existing responsibilities, and often some level of compromise is needed. We create our reality via our thoughts, beliefs, and vibration, so anything is possible, but often a balance must be struck. If you have three children but are too much of a free spirit to be confined to a job and want to go traveling around the world, then you need to consider some pros and cons.

> 'I began to prioritize the worthwhile over the meaningless. I realized that I wasn't actually contributing anything significant to the world or anybody else, apart from making a profit for my company so that my boss could drive an expensive car. My priorities were earning money, spending it, and going out at night. But as my awakening started, everything began to change. I decided to prioritize my health, skills, creativity, and making a difference over everything else. Now I'm a qualified Tai Chi instructor, and encourage people to learn about the Tao. My life is completely different, and I feel like I've found myself.'

You might begin to prioritize family over work, present-moment enjoyment over chasing future goals, and performing service to others over self-gratification. You may also start to shuffle your daily timetable, giving health, well-being, and other holistically beneficial activities more time and priority.

Preferences

Some things you used to like aren't as appealing anymore. Many people become vegetarian or vegan because they realize that animals are sentient too. You might clear out your kitchen cupboards and throw out all the salty, sugary, additive-filled, low-nutrition foods, replacing them with tasty, natural foods instead. You start reading nutrition labels, trying to make sure everything is as natural as possible.

> *'I have a selection of green powders that smell like the bottom of a boat, but they're some of the most nutritious foods in the world.'*

Chlorella, spirulina, kelp, wheatgrass, turmeric, lion's mane mushroom powder – you name it – they're ready to go into a nose-pinching liquid concoction, swallowed hastily for vibrant health. Celery juice for good digestion, pomegranate and grapeseed powder for antioxidants, and papaya seeds for micronutrients. Whatever combination of life-giving foods you choose, you're pleased with yourself, your new high vibration, and energy levels.

Your entertainment preference might divert from ultimately meaningless, fear-mongering, murderous, or trivial shows, toward more mind-expanding material. I still like to watch a movie or a series now and then, but considerably less than I used to, and I no longer watch regular television. Like many people, you might recycle your TV.

Now that you're moving into the reconstruction stages of awakening, you may prefer to live life to the fullest rather than laze on the couch. You realize that a human lifetime is a precious journey of learning and experience, and you want to make the most of it. Why do our preferences change? Like our priorities, the importance we give to things – some of which we may not have understood the significance of before – changes.

Perceptions

Perceptions are the way we interpret and understand the world, and they arise owing to beliefs and assumptions we have about it. Perceptions are like colored glasses that tint and shade how we see everything.

Before awakening, we might perceive children as little people we love and care for, but after awakening, they are wondrous soul consciousness, perhaps ageless and infinite. A tree might be a nice addition to our backyard, but after awakening, we begin to sense its energetic presence, strength, wisdom, and aliveness. We perceive it differently.

In realizing the oneness of all things, we begin to perceive others as part of us, Mother Earth as sacred, and reality as our playground to manifest as we see fit. We appreciate the profoundness and sanctity of all life, magnifying feelings of gratitude for all that we have and experience. We perceive mistakes as lessons to help us grow, people's gossip as meaningless and easy to transcend, and unfortunate events as opportunities to maintain our calmness.

Additionally, our relationship with the world changes completely once we understand that love is the way, and we, therefore, begin to see the world through new loving eyes. Our judgments soften, our reactions calm, and there is understanding where there was blame, forgiveness where there was resentment, and compassion where there was disregard. Love is the highest vibration and can heal all ills and distortions.

Personality

You might look back at your former self and see a different person. Imagine yourself as you were before awakening and ask yourself how you have changed. Your ego does affect your personality, but in all these fuzzy definitions, personality is partially separate. It's also your distinctiveness as an individual, what you're truly like as a person, your innate characteristics and qualities.

Upon awakening, you might feel and express more empathy for others, and this shines through in your personality. If someone were to describe you now, they might say that you have become a more compassionate, creative, and expressive person, more individual, different from 'normal' people. It's true that during awakening we experience individuation – we are no longer a replica of societal norms. Perhaps you're more confident in your own beingness; it's harder to foster confidence while maintaining an identity that isn't truly you.

You might occasionally feel angry during your awakening, or that the state of the world is making you bitter, or suspect that your personality has changed for the worse. After all, you've awoken as a spiritual being in a materially focused society under earthly illusions, so it's understandable to feel angry and overwhelmed. But we can try to release anger and frustration that the world doesn't seem to reflect our spiritual values; otherwise, we remain in an ongoing low vibration. What is it that's making you feel angry? How can you work through it? By taking calm action, rest assured that you are making a difference. We need to accept our anger to release it, realize that it is happening, then find constructive ways forward. When you are clearer about what you're willing to put up with, you're more likely to stand up for what's right and ethical, to maintain your boundaries, and speak out against injustice.

Profession

I discussed earlier how we can become disillusioned with our job if we feel it has no overriding purpose or benefit to others or the world, but a change of profession is not always necessary. You see, spiritually conscious individuals are needed in all professions and business sectors. Just because you have a spiritual awakening doesn't mean you have to become a Reiki healer or a yoga teacher, although these are beneficial professions. Who would provide dignified care in assisted living facilities, design eco-friendly buildings, or harvest organic kale?

As conscious, knowledgeable, loving individuals, we can make a difference in all areas of life, in any profession, even the financial industry! I mean, does it really need to make so much money? Perhaps spiritually conscious individuals can ethically influence decision-making so that central banks stop creating money out of thin air to be paid back at a substantial profit, and making people pay for their houses twice over via their mortgages.

We can bring spiritual values and ethics into industries that pollute the environment, exploit low-paid workers, and perhaps strive to transform our way of life through new political ideas. You might have the urge to change your job to one where you can express yourself better, help others, and make a difference, or even start your own venture. Whatever you do, be sure to follow your heart, joy, and intuition.

Pastimes

As awakening unfolds, and we move through the searching and seeking stage, a great many people retain a thirst for spiritual, esoteric, and metaphysical knowledge, and love to discuss it online, for example. Spiritual development might begin to dominate your spare time. Your creativity might also flow more easily as you strengthen your connection with higher aspects of self. Art, crafts, cooking, sculpture, poetry, writing, and music are some of the outlets for your energetic expression.

You might also spend more time in the forest, mountains, or by the sea, accommodating your deep connection with the natural world, replenishing your energies. And as many reduce their fears and anxieties through healing, they seek fresh experiences, perhaps enjoying more sport and travel.

Practices

There are heaps of practices we can do to help the mind, body, and spirit heal, ascend, and transform. Many attend courses on healing techniques such as Reiki, acupressure, acupuncture, hypnotherapy, tapping (EFT), homoeopathy, or reflexology, and learn spiritual skills such as past-life regression, divination, astrology, and numerology. In learning and performing these practices, we meet new friends at groups, seminars, and workshops, and some might be or become our clients. The loneliness phase can become a distant memory.

Meditation brings us closer to oneness and peacefulness, and helps us become aware of and heal our shadows. Yet, if we intend to, we can also attain trance states during meditation and perform journeying, astral projection, channeling, or commune with our guides and higher self. The urge to perform rituals and ceremonies can also be strong, indicating a shamanic leaning. You might gather herbs for natural remedies or cleansing with smoke, or develop an interest in plant medicine or altered states of consciousness. You may start group sessions using sound to cleanse and clear energies, working with drums, gongs, bells, and singing bowls.

Incorporating these practices into your life can mean a significant change for you and those around you. You're focusing your energies in constructive and useful directions, working with your innate knowing and remembering, bringing positive energies and ancient wisdom into this earthly reality.

People

Naturally, the people you choose to surround yourself with will change. Old friends might fall away because you have less in common with them, and new friends, with whom you resonate, enter your life. You might find there are not many likeminded people where you live, and sometimes there are none. Many clients of mine have said they live in predominantly religious towns or areas, where the inhabitants frown upon their spirituality. You can travel to meet new friends, relocate to another area, or make friends online; many people do these things. Take steps to remedy the situation or consider accepting it as a challenge. If it seems impossible now, then trust you'll find a solution. If you trust you'll meet new people, then that is what you will manifest. (I'll go into relating to others during awakening in more depth in Chapter 5.)

Purpose

The ninth life change is purpose. You may not have had one before, but if you did, it might not seem so worthwhile anymore. Now that most or all your other *p*'s are changing, and you're realizing your potential, you might be unable to contain your expression, creativity, gifts, and abilities, or at least the urge to find them! Some have a great deal of trouble finding their purpose, nothing quite seems to fit, or everything they want to do seems completely impossible. That's why I address finding your purpose in detail later on.

Seeking Healing

Have you ever met someone who maintains they are completely fine, even very happy, yet they are irritable, self-absorbed, jealous, obsessive, or some other distinct sort of unhelpful trait? They might be telling themselves that they are 'fine' because that's how they'd like to be, but obviously, they're not and are not very self-aware. Some are unwilling to face their shadows, those darker aspects of self that follow us around and can emerge as unpleasant emotions or destructive behaviors. But upon awakening, we realize it's more than acceptable to admit we are not doing so well or feeling very good, and at that moment, we take an enormous leap forward.

It's okay not to be okay, yet I urge you not to dwell in the shadows. Instead, congratulate yourself for recognizing them and agreeing to heal them. In Chapter 8, I'll provide methods for inner work healing, because this is one of the most important things we can do. Any recurring unpleasant emotion or unhelpful personality trait is an opportunity to do inner work to help you feel good ongoing. If you heal, your consciousness can move on and expand and grow. A significant part of inner work is listening to our pain, both emotional and physical, then accepting it and tracing it back to the source within our subconscious for healing.

Why does awakening inspire us to seek healing? From your higher self's point of view, both your positive and negative experiences are excellent catalysts for your expansion and growth. But beyond the experiences themselves, there is more to learn. We are completing only part of the challenge by merely *having* life experiences; we must also reexamine, understand, forgive, reconcile, and heal them before we, well, win. And the prize is a naturally higher vibration.

🦋 EXERCISE: RAISE YOUR VIBRATION 🦋

You can reprogram your subconscious mind through repetition when you are in a relaxed state. The subconscious mind accepts new beliefs when you repeat them to yourself. Now, this is only a temporary solution, because if you need inner work (and most people do) that you're not performing, then old beliefs are likely to take root again. Affirmations are wonderful to use in conjunction with inner work and can provide a quick high vibrational pick-me-up too. We must always frame affirmations in the positive lest the subconscious retain the negative word. I often see them framed incorrectly. So 'I am love and compassion' is acceptable, but 'I release pain and sadness' is not. You don't want to program your subconscious mind with 'pain' and 'sadness.'

Choose one of the following affirmations and remember it. Use one affirmation per session.

~ I am love and compassion.

~ I am a free, powerful, sovereign being.

~ I am happiness, and I am joy.

~ Abundance is everywhere, and it enters my life easily.

~ I find peace and balance in all situations.

~ I love and accept myself for who I am.

~ I welcome courage, confidence, and prosperity.

~ I have gratitude for all that I have and will receive.

~ I forgive myself and others, and welcome love into my heart.

1. Make sure you'll be undisturbed, then sit quietly and close your eyes.

2. Observe your breath for about 10 minutes. Try to breathe rhythmically, comfortably, and deeply into your belly rather than your chest. Pace your breathing in such a way so as not to make yourself dizzy.

3. Feel and listen to the air going in and out, and experience your belly rising and falling. If thoughts come, allow them to float away gently.

4. After the 10 minutes, prepare to listen to your own voice intently.

5. Repeat your affirmation out loud, between breaths, for about five minutes. Say your affirmation at a slow pace, then take a slow deep breath in and out. Repeat the affirmation slowly again, then take another slow deep breath in and out. Repeat the cycle.

6. Thank your subconscious mind (we want to make friends with ourselves), and open your eyes when you're ready.

Settling In

As the whirlwind of awakening calms, you begin to settle into your spiritual journey, and this may happen in weeks, months, or even a couple of years after your initial triggering event. You're entering the reintegration stage, also known as the embodiment phase, which can feel a lot like coming home.

As we settle into our new priorities, routines and, self, our inner world calms, and we see both the ugliness and beauty of the outer world more clearly – what contrasts it has. We've already had many shocking realizations, and now there are fewer to be had all at once. In a way, we become a little desensitized to the out-of-the-ordinary because we are becoming used to it. Metaphysical, esoteric, or other hidden knowledge stands to reason rather than seeming unbelievable or mind-blowing.

Most likely, you'll still go through tough times – we all do. After all, you are incarnate as a human being, and that means there will be challenges. Your higher self still wants you to experience occasional difficulties so that you will learn and grow. Besides, if you never experienced difficulties, you wouldn't know what happiness is because you'd have nothing to compare it to. Happiness is more potent when you've endured the complete opposite. Tough times can also lead you in a better direction, because challenges catalyze us to take affirmative action. Problems are sometimes blessings in disguise.

❛ The truth is, everything will be okay as soon
as you are okay with everything. And that's
the only time everything will be okay.❜
MICHAEL A. SINGER

Allow life to wash over you like water running off a duck's back. Whatever life throws my way, I let it wash over me, remaining unruffled by unfortunate circumstances and bathing in the enjoyable ones. I give myself the benefit of the doubt, knowing I have a certain level of intelligence and ability, so, along with my intuition, I give myself space to figure out the best way forward. If we release resistance to life, Creation senses our higher vibration and gives us happier circumstances because that's what we most need for our learning and experience.

Awakening Settles, Yet the Journey Continues

Awakening has given you answers to some burning questions. You have tools for self-development and ways to work toward contentment. You also have a pocket full of inspiration and lots of potential for its use. You know you'll be okay, because you are still here, still breathing, and the sky hasn't fallen. Moments of profound realization will continue to arrive throughout your journey; even if there are months of seemingly little significant progress or exciting developments, you'll suddenly figure out something new about yourself, which will completely change how you feel yet again.

The more authentic you become, the more you can relax. It's arduous to pretend to be something you're not. When you were a kid, you were probably carefree, felt full of confidence, and followed your enthusiasm at every opportunity. Then others and perhaps life took quite a bit of those feelings away. It's time to remember what it was like to be a child expressing your joy. So relax and take some time to talk to your inner child who is still within you. They might help you remember all the things you used to find exciting.

Your Heart Opens

The following example illustrates how many people sadly learn the vibration of fear and therefore, hatred, while growing up.

> 'As a teenager, I used to walk past homeless people and think negatively of them, as if I were great, and they were small. I had a horrible attitude of objection toward them, which I learned from my family. One day, during my awakening, I realized that being homeless was not a life choice and that all humans deserve to have their needs for safety, comfort, and well-being met. I couldn't believe I had accepted such attitudes and felt new, out-of-this-world love and compassion for those in need.'

Awakening shows us the way back to love. In bringing love into your life as a foundation for everything you do, think, or say, your reality changes. If you are confused, think of the most loving explanation. If you're passing judgment, ask what love would decide. If you're dealing with other people, allow love to guide you. I have found that in doing this, life unfolds like a carpet of light under your feet, things fall into place, and people are kind in return.

> *We have been brought up in a world that does not put love first, and where love is absent, fear sets in. Fear is to love as darkness is to light.*
> MARIANNE WILLIAMSON

In welcoming love, we receive the light. We can begin to accept and listen to our fears; in resisting them, they remain self-perpetuating. Worrying about what *might* happen is our fear of fear. We literally fear being in fear. You can tell yourself not to, but it persists because it just happens whether you like it or not. So, in being present with your fears, you no longer create the worry-resistance, and your emotions feel heard and comforted.

In having such knowledge and perceptual changes like the example just illustrated, your feelings begin to change. You are integrating the wisdom you're learning, and your mind, body, and spirit are settling into a comfortable daily rhythm. There is a difference between knowing, understanding, and embodying spiritual wisdom. You can't rush these progressions; they happen naturally as your mind creates pathways and connections back and forth between information, experience, meaning, and all their implications. Knowing is not always understanding, especially on a deep enough level to be able to live it.

Knowing, Understanding, and Embodying

Let's explore for a moment this process of knowing, understanding, and embodying. It's a holistic approach to wholeness. You read something profound, which has the potential to change your perceptions enough to impact your reality. Yet, knowing the information is only the first level. You grasp the golden nugget of information, but without time for your subconscious mind to integrate it into the context of your life, you can't always truly understand its implications. You'll have experiences in the future when your new realization comes in handy, at which point, you begin to understand how it applies to you. Even greater understanding occurs when you apply it to past, present, *and* future events. Now you are embodying the wisdom as you work it through your very being, living it, using it, and practicing it. You're developing greater emotional and felt intelligence. This process continues onward through life, and each time you become wiser, more skillful, and balanced. Your spiritual path is settling into a journey of contemplation and psychological discoveries relevant to you. You're walking the walk, not just talking the talk. In esoteric circles, this process is known as *gnosis*, meaning lived, experienced knowledge.

~

Chapter 5

Facing Family, Friends, and Everyday Life

Whether we have a good relationship with our family or a less than supportive one, during awakening most of us experience at least some sort of disconnect from them, our partners, friends, or workmates, no matter how solid the relationships are.

Reactions from Family and Friends

The trouble is, most of them don't remotely understand what you're going through, because awakening is simply not within their frame of reference. People often fear what they don't understand, and as they have little or no understanding of the concepts you're trying to convey, they become concerned. Cognitive dissonance immediately kicks in for your beloved family members because your words contradict their version of reality; your words do not compute. People reject or attempt to explain away everything you say, and often won't even listen to you. Your words make them uneasy because their reality feels nice and safe as it is, and you're jeopardizing that. Sometimes they are understandably alarmed because many of us do experience significant emotional upheaval, incoherent thought, or become physically unwell during awakening. But frequently, interactions present further pain because you're being shut down by the people you hold most dear, for expressing what's most important to you. You believe the concepts you're espousing should be significant to them, too, but usually, they just aren't.

> *'I visited my parents, and my sister was there. I tried to tell them about some of the things I've been researching, because I felt they needed to know. I explained that because you can't patent or profit much from plants in their natural form, it's not in the pharmaceutical industry's interest to promote natural remedies. All three of them acted as if I was a danger to society. So I decided to lighten the mood by telling them how I've been studying a form of Chinese divination called the I Ching, which I have found exceptionally insightful. They looked at me as if I'd gone insane. I decided to shut up. My dad told me to get my head out of the clouds; my sister made a joke out of it; and my mother is now worried about me. I feel pretty resentful toward them now.'*

It's understandable to feel embarrassed, misunderstood, or resentful. Some families are more open and understanding, but some can behave harshly. But in developing understanding and empathy for them, we can learn to forgive them. From their point of view, you're acting strangely, you're not yourself; therefore, something must be wrong. Yet all you want to do is offer them knowledge you feel would be beneficial to them. People often fear change and uncertainty because they feel they are losing control. Your family usually know what to expect from you, and they didn't expect you to say the things you are, or for you to be experiencing the emotional difficulty of an awakening they might even perceive as dangerous. They feel like they are losing the person they love. They loved you as you were, and now you're seemingly becoming a stranger.

We all want to be validated, accepted, and loved, and often we grow up believing that love is conditional. The conditions are that if you perform positive actions, you receive acknowledgment, love, and praise, and if you behave poorly or even make a mistake, love is withdrawn. Therefore, approaching our family can be an emotionally risky task because of potential rejection, ridicule, and the loss of their support. Sometimes though, our family surprises us, so do give them the benefit of the doubt. They may react negatively at first, but given time, can warm up. This is what it was like for me.

Experiencing Harsh Rejection

Those who have a strong religious background often have an especially tough time, though. Religious family members tend to perceive your interests and practices as evil or demonic. The level of rejection is often fiercer than that from a family of atheists, who are less likely to think your actions are dangerous and more likely to think you are just being silly. Either way, it feels pretty awful. Many clients have told me of being unable to shake feelings of guilt, shame, or wrongdoing when they're performing meditation, yoga, divination, energy healing, or even using crystals. If you have chosen to move on from the religion you grew up with, then you are exhibiting your ability for independent thought, illustrating your strength of character. You don't need permission to continue to exercise your free will, and you're not doing anything wrong. If you want to meditate, for example, it's likely you already know in your heart that it's beneficial. Otherwise, you wouldn't feel so drawn to do it.

We do tend to tolerate more from our family than we would from other people from whom we'd be more likely to cut ties. Although tolerance and acceptance are crucial principles many, including myself, live by, when we allow others to violate our boundaries, we are inadvertently teaching them how to treat us. It's in our best interest to make clear what's acceptable and what is not. We can perhaps tolerate and accept that they might overreact or laugh at us at first, but abuse or continual teasing is not acceptable.

I always recommend working on family relationships, and I'll explain how shortly. However, if you experience rejection and derision, consider distancing yourself for a while. You may already have the urge to do so. If any relationships are continually unpleasant, controlling, manipulative, or destructive to you, then this is likely the best course of action. We often need to go inward and spend time alone during awakening. Unhelpful reactions from others are not conducive to your healing and overall healthy emergence from the process. If your family is not willing to help you after you've explained your emotions, and they show no signs of softening over time, then they may be doing you more harm than good. You need to protect yourself, especially during this time in which you might be in a vulnerable state. Consider seeking support elsewhere.

You may feel like shouting from the rooftops, letting everybody know of your discoveries, but, although the urge to do so is strong, you can't awaken everybody. Everyone has their own beliefs, even if their religion is materialist science or their church the shopping mall. Naturally, you know that the spiritual path is not one of preaching or recruiting people; most of us offer knowledge when appropriate or drop little seeds of thought.

You might try to tell your friends of your spiritual realizations, only to have them rebuff you with a look of confusion or a *Why are you being weird?* facial expression. Some of your friends will fight to protect the paradigm they're in, so they'll argue against anything outside of it. You might find these friends naturally fall away.

Some Will Stay, Some Will Go

Awakening shows us the friends who will be eternally present, and those who will vanish into thin air. In a way, the whole process illustrates who our true friends really are. Those who have a severe dependency on their version of reality, now that you don't fit in with it, might not need you anymore. So perhaps their rejection is a gift in disguise. One day, they might contact you for help in figuring out some spiritual, metaphysical, or hidden-truth-related mystery. They may recall how you changed and know you're the person to consult in such matters. You may not want to assist them, but in doing so, you'll transcend past events and assume the highest vibration, that of love, compassion, and forgiveness.

Try not to feel hurt or guilty if some friends fall away. They might not be able to deal with the person you're becoming, because their frame of reference doesn't equip them to understand. Their backgrounds may not have prepared them or given them the strength to do so. Everyone behaves the way they do for a reason, and their past programming and experiences contribute significantly to who they are. Through this understanding, you can forgive them for drifting away. If the friendship ends, perhaps it wasn't supposed to continue and wasn't for your highest good. You may also worry that by distancing yourself from friends during your hermit or isolating phase, they will resent you for not making contact. You can't force yourself to socialize but can explain that you are going through some emotional challenges and leave it at that. Again, you must do what's right for you. Likely, the best of your friends will still be there once you reemerge from the process.

Relationships Can and Do Improve

Friendships can actually be better after awakening, even old ones. Once you've become a more integrated and authentic version of yourself, you'll likely feel more at peace, confident, able to enjoy yourself, and be even better company for others.

For example, inner work has reduced my social anxiety by, I'd say, about 90 per cent, so spending time with friends and acquaintances is far more enjoyable for me, and this reflects in my behavior. My friends seem to relax more too. Awakening helps us express our emotions more freely, open up, and be vulnerable. When we share personal thoughts and stories more freely, we connect with others on a deeper level, and they are more inclined to share with us, too, strengthening friendships. Many of your friends might find that, even though for a while you were acting pretty far-out (by their standards), you're actually more awesome now.

Sometimes, perhaps after months, depending on the closeness of your relationships, your friends and family start to see that there is nothing to fear, you are *essentially* still you, and they begin to accept, or at least tolerate, your new way of thinking. They might even realize that the things you speak of actually hold truth. Remember, by worrying about you, they are showing they care. If usually kind individuals change for the worse, it's worth giving them time to adjust. Although it feels like they're rejecting you, often their reactions are coming from a place of fear within themselves. Their intolerance of the person you're becoming has a lot to do with their own insecurities. You can reassure them that you haven't gotten into anything sinister or dangerous and that the changes you're going through are ultimately good. I told my family that I was particularly enjoying learning about Buddhism, psychology, and well-being, and they instantly relaxed because they could understand and relate to these things. Such topics do, after all, make a significant contribution to our spiritual understandings.

The Opinionated Uncle

Awakening makes the thought patterns of friends and family very apparent, now that you are stepping outside of them and looking in. Beliefs, values, and attitudes that you had all your life display like writing on the wall. You see your old self and your previous version of 'normal' in them and realize how much you have changed.

> *'I went for Christmas dinner, and my uncle was there. I used to find him funny, but now his jokes seem thoughtless, intolerant, and sometimes racist. It was very difficult to sit there and listen without saying anything. I imagined myself protesting, and then everyone piping up and saying that I was the one with the bad attitude, accusing me of ruining the day. So I said nothing, but I couldn't wait to get out of there.'*

It doesn't take an awakening to gain awareness of tolerance, unity, and compassion, but these are certainly realizations that come with it. It can be challenging to endure seemingly unloving modes of thought once we're moving toward oneness and unity. In such circumstances, the blissfulness we have been fostering vanishes. Unless we change our approach, that is. I'll explain shortly.

Relating to Family and Friends

If you recall what you were like before your awakening and all the earthly beliefs and assumptions you had, you can see things from your family's of point of view. If a loved one had come to you in the throes of awakening, would you have experienced resistance or felt concerned? Maybe yes, maybe no, but with this kind of understanding, you can release some of your resentment, humiliation, or annoyance about their reactions toward you.

Understanding, Forgiveness, and Calmness

As with the example of the opinionated uncle, we can reach a state where we are relatively emotionally unaffected by their response, while we remain aware of the distastefulness of the situation. We can, therefore, take calm action to maintain our boundaries or to protest their remarks peacefully. Unpleasant emotion is, well, unpleasant, but in such a situation, we create far better outcomes by keeping a calm and stable demeanor. We can do this by imagining what kind of background or backstory the person has. What has led them to hold such attitudes? It may be their upbringing, their community, their experiences, or historical family attitudes. They might not even realize the ramifications of their words, having never thought to empathize with you or others or to see beyond what they have learned to repeat. In this way, we see that many people are a product of an unquestioned past, having never learned to empathize or have compassion. This kind of understanding releases much resentment, because we realize they could do with some inner healing and awareness, like all of us to varying degrees. I'm not implying that being on the spiritual path always makes us right. But at least we can, through understanding and, therefore, forgiveness, calmly discuss with others our loving and tolerant point of view without becoming agitated ourselves.

Working through Friction

Your beliefs, priorities, and values are moving out of alignment with others', and this natural metamorphic process is taking you to the fringes of thought, not a place where your family and friends reside. You might, therefore, still inadvertently find yourself in a disagreement or even a full-blown argument. But sometimes, in airing 'negative' energies and emotions, much is cleared. If there is a tremendous falling-out, then perhaps you can all start afresh afterward.

What about when someone pessimistically dismisses or argues against your new spiritual ideas, practices, and principles? Should you simply put up with it? Or is there a balanced approach to take? At the beginning of my awakening, I would argue back but found it fueled the fire of emotions within all of us even more. Nowadays, I'll happily and calmly disagree, even persistently, but not mind about the outcome. I've transcended the need to convince anyone of anything and, therefore, released the frustrations that come with it. Who says I am absolutely right anyway? I can only try my best and offer my point of view. I always enjoy any civil discussion, but if it becomes unpleasant, I'll remove myself from the debate, emotionally unmoved because people will always think what they wish.

More often than not, if we change ourselves within, others change. I'm not saying change yourself for the benefit of others, but amend your attitudes and approach. We can do this through understanding, acceptance, and forgiveness.

> 'My mother and I didn't always get along. She would judge
> me all the time, and I was often offended by her remarks.
> So we would fight. It was much worse once my awakening
> began. But then I had a perceptual shift and realized why
> she says the things she does. I became aware that, although
> she has a knack of framing comments in ways that seem
> abrupt or tactless, she's essentially speaking from a place of
> love. Through my new understanding, my reactions toward
> her softened, and her opinions no longer annoyed me.
> Then, because I was much calmer and kinder around her,
> she became pleasant and more loving around me too.'

I know of many such instances where people have changed their
attitudes and approaches to others with the same results, and in
this mind-set, spending time with family during awakening can
become much more enjoyable.

Loved ones and friends may eventually accept the person you
are becoming, so allow them time. Until then, set the intention
to release sensitivity to others' judgments because they cannot
dictate who you are; that is for you to decide. When others frame
criticism constructively, of course, it's best to take on board all
that might, in fact, be beneficial to you. But bear in mind that
judgments of you regarding your spiritual or alternative interests
are quite likely biased and misinformed.

Shall I Be Me or the Old Me?

We tend to create two versions of ourselves, two personas.
While one is traversing the awakening process, we maintain the

other, somewhat obsolete version, to fit in and keep the peace with our family and friends. But how beneficial is it to filter or change yourself?

> 'About a month into my awakening, I began to feel like I had two separate personalities, one which was still changing and developing, and another I'd put on to fit in with other people. I learned pretty quickly what their reactions would be when I talked about spirituality. So I wore the old version of myself like a mask with everyone, especially my workmates, for fear of them rejecting me. I still do it to this day. I don't want to go on like this; I can't be myself.'

At first, we need time to find and settle into our new self, so presenting a persona reduces the chances of rejection and disagreements *and* our associated unpleasant emotions. In the early stages, it's a delicate situation for us. But are we not striving for authenticity? Shouldn't we just *be* ourselves? I suggest that it is your choice, if needed, to filter your words and behaviors. If you are consciously choosing to do this to maintain your well-being during awakening, then you are indeed being authentic. A conscious decision is a genuine one because you are not simply unconsciously reacting to stimuli. So if you mindfully decide to present as your 'normal' old self for a time, try not to feel like you're doing anything 'wrong.' You're just doing what you need to do. Over time, you'll gain more confidence in being your genuine self, and require less and less the acceptance and validation of those who don't accept you for who you are.

Therefore, motivation to maintain the pre-awakening version of yourself gradually diminishes.

When you are feeling stronger, having traveled along your spiritual path for some time, you'll be in a perfect position to begin your *light work*: You can gently raise the vibration of those around you with helpful tips on self-care, wellness, and healing dotted with mind-expanding ideas. Your energy, too, will make a subconscious difference to the vibration of others. You may find it's best not to come out with anything too esoteric or mystical to those who are closed off to it. Many light bringers choose what to share and with whom with great skill. It can mean the difference between making a significant contribution to their well-being or having them back off completely. Many of us have learned this the hard way. Some people might be open to mindfulness but not to connecting with their higher self. They may think inner healing is an excellent idea, but energy work utterly preposterous. The skill lies in being able to empathize with the person you're speaking to, understanding their personal paradigm, and to what they can relate. Drop little seeds of thoughts if you intuitively feel they will benefit from them. The seeds may take root and grow later on.

I had a good clear-out of friends on social media and felt liberated. I somewhat regret it now, though, because I am more confident in who I am, but at the time it was necessary. I made new friends with whom I could be myself, but it felt like being in an echo chamber. I feel it's vital to still have plenty of contact with people outside spiritual and conscious circles to remain in touch with 3D, earthly life and remember what it was like before awakening. Therefore, we maintain empathy for all. We are *one* with *all* people, not just the spiritual community. But remember to contemplate releasing guilt for separating yourself from those who judge you or behave negatively or harshly. You can choose who you want in your life for your highest good.

Emotionally Hooked on Them

If your family and friends continue to be a source of emotional turbulence, you might be especially dependent on and, therefore, unduly vulnerable to their responses and opinions. We are affected by them only because they poke at parts of our psyche that are sensitive. Energetic or emotional cords of attachment are essentially cords of light that connect us with another person. They form as we create bonds, love, or depend on them. In cutting the cords, we sever this connection and become less emotionally influenced by their actions. It doesn't mean we don't love or want to see them anymore; instead, we are becoming more energetically whole and complete. We also release old drama, resentment, and karma surrounding these relationships. We can start anew.

EXERCISE: CUTTING EMOTIONAL CORDS OF ATTACHMENT

In this practice, you're reducing how much another person affects your well-being. This process uses visualization. Remember, if this is tricky for you, you can sense or just know what is going on.

1. Make sure you'll be undisturbed and sit or lie in a comfortable position.

2. Focus on your breath for about 20 minutes and allow every part of your body to relax.

3. Visualize a person from whom you'd like to cut emotional cords of attachment. Allow them to come to mind, standing in front of you.

4. Become aware of any cords of energy linking you to them. They may be silvery or gold in color. There may be more than one attached to different areas on the body.

5. Tell the person, either mentally or out loud, that you are releasing attachment from them today.

6. In your mind's eye, begin to pull the cords from your body. They release easily and painlessly.

7. As they separate from your body, they begin to dissolve from end to end.

8. Remove them all and observe them dissolving until they disappear.

9. Be aware that this action signifies releasing your attachment to the person's judgments and actions.

10. Thank the person and wish them love.

11. Relax for a few moments and then open your eyes when you're ready.

Your Intimate Relationship

Those undergoing awakening tell of all sorts of reactions from their partners. Some are surprisingly open to listening and ultimately begin agreeing with you. Others find conscious and metaphysical concepts mildly amusing or entertaining without minding too much. Yet others distance themselves while disdainfully tolerating it. And finally, there are those who kick up a terrible fuss, refuting such nonsense, contemptuously ridiculing you at every opportunity. Since it's more stressful than it's worth to mention your new crystals or your highly synchronous afternoon, you keep your interests to yourself.

You both fell in love with each other's personalities and everything that makes you who you are, but now one of you is changing. As you transform and grow, you may no longer desire a partner who reflects your old mind-set, and your partner might end up missing your former self who was more like them. They are wondering who this stranger is and where their partner has gone.

We tend to manifest relationships that reflect who we are at the time, our core beliefs, and the vibration we are holding. If we are lonely, we tend to attract a partner who makes us feel alone in their presence or will abandon us. If we dislike ourselves, we'll manifest someone who fills us with self-loathing. If we fear losing our freedom, we'll manifest a jealous and overprotective partner. You attract partners according to your thoughts, beliefs, and vibration because that must be what you need for your learning and experience.

Nurturing a Conscious Relationship

What is a conscious relationship? I define it as a mutually beneficial relationship where both individuals are committed to loving, supporting, and understanding one another, while mindfully assisting in each other's personal and spiritual growth. If you're both committed to each other's growth and well-being while agreeing to perform ongoing inner work and self-development, then you have the makings of a highly supportive and fulfilling relationship.

Every relationship is a mirror. Each partner shows the other many things about themselves through the stirring of emotions, both pleasant and unpleasant. We can reflect on our responses, reactions, behaviors, and bodily sensations, if and when the other person catalyzes them. As a result, opportunities for healing arise because we realize where we are having trouble handling or dealing with things. Where there is overreaction, there might be a hidden, painful wound, although keep in mind that there is actually no such thing as an overreaction because everyone reacts the way they do for a reason. We usually find the reason in unfavorable past circumstances and trauma or unacceptable ongoing present circumstances. Hence, we attempt to locate the source of distress, heal the wounds, or change the circumstances. Partners have the power to bring out both the best and worst in us; therefore, we find sources of joy to follow and causes of pain to heal. However, your partner might be downright resistant to conscious self-development and be unwilling to heal and reflect.

That's why some relationships don't make it through awakening. Those that survive do so because both partners are open and willing to listen and adjust. Their vibrations remain aligned, and occasionally, one awakens the other. Both continue to manifest each other's presence and commitment and even mutually accelerate the awakening process. However, if both partners are at odds, the ever-increasing vibrational misalignment literally manifests each other out of their respective realities. In addition, the partner who is transforming may begin to attract, or draw to them, a different kind of friend, acquaintance, or potential partner, often those on the path of healing and self-discovery who better align with their thoughts, beliefs, and vibration. Therefore, they are more likely to meet new people who, in contrast to their partner, are refreshingly different and stimulating, and similar to themselves. Perhaps their soulmate or perfect vibrational equivalent will enter their life.

Needs and Boundaries Can Change

Awakening can show us that our relationship is unacceptable. What we deemed normal is, in fact, intolerable, and we realize we have been suffering needlessly. During this self-empowering process and call to authenticity, we begin to set healthier boundaries or consider ending the unhealthy relationship.

> 'I grew up in quite neglectful circumstances, and when anyone would bother to talk to me, they would belittle and mock me. Unfortunately, I ended up thinking this kind of treatment was normal, and all that I could expect from people was more of the same. Somehow, every relationship I entered would be destructive, unhealthy, and disrespectful. Okay, I get it now. I was probably

> *manifesting these people due to my limiting beliefs, and that seems pretty unfair. But I'd stay in the relationships for years before leaving because I thought this was how relationships were supposed to be. It's different now that I've realized my self-worth, increased my self-love, and changed my expectations. I seem to meet far fewer people like that, and wouldn't put up with it anyway.'*

If your relationship is continually making you unhappy, consider new futures. A moment will arrive when you're sure your efforts with your partner are futile. Your nine *p*'s are likely changing. Can your partner tolerate and accept all that? You might require support, especially during the initial stages of awakening. Is your partner helpful? Or are they exacerbating the situation seemingly unnecessarily?

> *'I tried to keep my relationship going after my awakening. I loved her and didn't want to let go. But we had nothing in common anymore, and she thinks that my astrology work is nonsense and that veganism will make me ill. She doesn't listen to or understand me at all, and I can no longer relate to her. I knew I needed to spend time healing so that I could find my energetic equilibrium.'*

If the relationship ends, it doesn't mean it was all for nothing or a waste of time. As with all relationships, whether happy and loving or hurtful and destructive, they're all experiences from which we learn and grow. So if you're in a relationship that's suffering due to your awakening, what should you do? You can't force your partner to change, and you can't make them awaken. They might when they are ready, but only might.

Should I Convince My Partner to Pursue the Spiritual Path?

Your partner probably holds a myriad of perceptions that actively prevent them from realizing the infinite, energetic nature of self and reality. They may perceive the existence of spirit, or life after death, as totally fanciful and naive. How big a task do you think it will be to convince them otherwise? And is it really up to you (or anyone else) to convince anyone of anything? They must choose to accept alternative perceptions themselves, having examined enough evidence or experienced personal proof. They'll put up even more resistance if you are forcing ideas on them. Help them to understand your transformation, but it's best not to overload them with spiritual concepts and ideas, lest cognitive dissonance kick in, and they reject everything you say. Allow them to accept the person you are becoming at their own pace.

I tend to focus on ways to preserve relationships because, although awakening can make life tough at first, the situation can improve. If you were to break up at the first sign of resistance, you might miss out on the transformation your partner *could* have. Even the most materially minded person can have a spiritual awakening triggered by their partner. But your intuition must play a role. If you feel that the relationship is destined to end, then follow your feelings. We often stay in relationships for many logical reasons without actually following our heart and joy.

Your relationship might improve as you continue your path of healing and begin to perceive the situation with more love and understanding. The relationship might actually be better than before due to your awakening. Every relationship responds differently, so give your partner the benefit of the doubt, especially if you love them. It might take six months or more to gauge whether or not you'll both be able to realign vibrationally.

Communication and Connection

You don't have to share all your interests, but your partner should at least be tolerating and accepting of your new beliefs. Excellent communication is key. Help them to understand why you are performing new practices, why your diet is changing, your reasons for meditating, contemplating, and reading this special genre of material. Help them recognize that you're on a journey of self-exploration and growth and that there's nothing to fear.

Give each other space but set time aside to connect in some of the ways you used to or to explore new shared interests. They might like some of the pastimes and activities you suggest. There's nothing like fun times to help. Try doing something together where there's less need to interact, especially if there's tension, like hiking in nature, a sporting activity, even the theater or bowling. Forcing yourself to socialize over dinner in a restaurant may result in more awkwardness, exacerbating your lack of connection. But having fun experiences together can reset your feelings, enabling healthier communication later.

If you find that your partner begins the awakening process, too, then perhaps your souls agreed to continue to evolve and grow together, and it was your job to awaken first. If your partner is open and willing, they may indeed entrain to your leading vibration, and you might automatically trigger their metamorphosis. It's like being two tuning forks. If you strike one, the other begins to resonate at the same frequency. Two minds that are closely linked react in the same way, as long as there aren't excessive layers of resistance toward each other.

❦ EXERCISE: HEALING COMMUNICATION ❦

Even if your partner has no interest in spirituality, the following exercise might still be acceptable to them as it is merely a practice for resolving challenges and conflict and for improving communication. It's never worth *making* them do it, instead encourage them to participate, with the reassurance that it might help you both. Be mindful to stay calm, centered, and understanding, even if your partner is becoming emotional. You can set the emotional tone.

1. Aim for understanding and agreement. Pick one challenging issue *each* so that you address two in each sitting.

2. Choose who goes first and start with their issue or difficulty. Focus only on that one. Be open to reaching an understanding and agreement. Remember that compromise is often necessary if relationships are to move forward.

3. Both of you complete each of the following sentences, even if the difficulty belongs to the other person. Take a turn to complete each one, then move on to the next.

~ Our relationship is important to me because

_____

~ I find this difficulty challenging because

_____

(If it is not challenging for one person, they may say so.)

~ It makes me feel

_____

~ I can help the situation by

_____

(Name as many solutions as possible.)

~ You can also help the situation by

_____

~ I am willing to compromise by

_____

~ I will support you further by

_____

4. Move on to the other partner's difficulty and work through the steps again.

5. Thank each other.

6. Allow at least a couple of days before performing the entire process again, each person having one new difficulty ready to address (if there is one).

Reintegrating with the World: The Journey Home

What happens when it's time to reintegrate with society during or after our transformation? Many individuals receive no respite and have to go to work throughout the process. How can we rejoin our community and resume everyday life when our nine *p*'s have shifted so much?

Consciousness Rising at Work

Your workplace can seem like a 3D cartoon where people expend copious amounts of energy on things you're not taking as seriously anymore. It can seem like a cosmic joke. But from their perspective, their actions are important to them, and you can be understanding of that. Practically speaking, you can meditate at lunchtime, perhaps in the park, to help you to rest and find balance. Your favorite crystal, depending on the type, can absorb or protect from unpleasant energies. Hold it or put it in your pocket. Just knowing it's there can help, and remember to wash it at least daily. A luscious green potted plant can help calm the energies in a busy office and keep you connected with Mother Earth. A cleansing salt bath after work will draw out unhelpful energies accumulated during the day. Two cups of Epsom, Himalayan or sea salt added to a warm bath should do the trick.

You might be the type of person who cares a lot about what people think, so in feeling different from others, shame might arise. How can you participate in workmates' conversations and find common ground? Many classify spiritual and mystical experiences as fanciful, ignorant, or irrational, so you can try to impersonate your old self (which can be tiring), authentically choose to filter, or be your true self completely. See what feels right to you. It's probably best to work toward genuinely being your true self around all people, over time, of course.

> '*I was shy about who I had become, but now I'm proud. At work, as I walked through the office and factory floor doing my duties, I observed many people from different backgrounds, Hindu, Muslim, atheist, and agnostic, all generally accepting of each other. Why shouldn't they accept me? It hit me just then that I should be proud of myself, and just as I accept others, I should accept myself. I had been worrying unnecessarily. Some of them actually shared my same beliefs or had meaningful spiritual experiences but never spoke of them.*'

One of the best things to do is own your spirituality and be proud; then shame tends to melt away. If we don't own it, then we are living in constant resistance to ourselves.

Reintegrating with the World

The main challenge is being able to function in a world that seems unreal. Advertising, consumerism, media, trends, politics, economics, gossip, controversy, and much more can seriously shatter your newfound, or nearly found, state of bliss and interconnectedness.

You *can* choose to isolate yourself, live in a monastery, or go out to the remote countryside to nurture your connection with the divine. You can find means to separate from society long-term if this is your desire for your ultimate spiritual growth. You'll still be serving the collective consciousness and holding space for humanity while diving deep into your inner world, the natural world, or spiritual wisdom. Alternatively, you can choose another path, one of sharing and connection, and if you do, it's best done with conviction and intention. You can be in the world but not *of* it. Having trust in Creation also helps – trust that all will be well, and then this is what you will manifest.

A bodhisattva is someone who returns to society to practice for the benefit of all. They help others achieve a state of peace, balance, and enlightenment similar to their own, and they share wisdom and understanding of the nature of things so that all can reach an infinite state of awareness. Boddhisattvas come in many forms: office and retail workers, construction workers, conservationists, and politicians, to name a few. Yes, ordinary people and sometimes even politicians!

> The idea of the Bodhisattva is the one who out
> of his realization of transcendence participates
> in the world. The imitation of Christ is joyful
> participation in the sorrows of the world.
>
> JOSEPH CAMPBELL

Rejoining society with the intention of helping others to find inner peace and understanding of the spiritual universe is a tremendous calling indeed. With this conviction, we choose to participate in the world for the greater good, we are optimistic in times of struggle, and guide others in transcending societal illusions. Endurance becomes part of our character, enabling us to support others through their sorrowful experiences. If you see yourself as a bodhisattva (another word for it is shaman), then go for it! Many are needed for humankind to flourish. This kind of path also solves the 'What is my purpose?' puzzle, if you're struggling to find it.

The carriers of the shamanic archetype leave the ordinary world and enter spiritual dimensions through awakening. When they eventually return, they bring knowledge of the infinite and divine back with them. Their skill rests in translating and verbalizing that knowledge for others in ways they are fascinated to hear and can effortlessly understand. If you resonate with this description, the shamanic archetype may be an intrinsic part of your energetic code.

You may never become a 'normal' citizen again, and you might need to accept that. You may always feel you are somehow different from the majority. Nevertheless, we must always be mindful and remember that we are not separate from others. We are one, and there are many who simply view the world through a different lens. Only our perceptions are different, not our essence. They, too, are infinite soul consciousness, each and every one; they just haven't remembered it yet.

Keeping these things in mind, you can begin to reintegrate with society. It's an internal process that takes time and tolerance, and definitely patience. We can develop patience through practice. We will always have workmates, neighbors, and acquaintances, unless we ourselves leave society. Therefore, it's beneficial to accept their continued presence. Understanding and patience calm our frustrations, for we remember what it was like to see through their eyes. We begin to thrive once we have acceptance and tolerance for all their points of view, and perhaps, we can take on the role of the shaman, healer, or bodhisattva.

Until we have found our authentic self, mingling with our community or workmates can still present emotional challenges. The following exercise can help a great deal, although it's more of a perceptual change than a practice. It's all about focusing on one particular concept throughout the day. The chosen concept is like a colored lens through which to view everything. With this shift in mind-set, you experience circumstances entirely differently, enabling you to stand tall in your own beingness and move through each day with intention and purpose.

🦋 Exercise: Concept of the Day 🦋

Perceptions color and create your reality. You might go to work, a social event, or anywhere else, carrying a lot of resistance for various reasons. Select one or more of the following concepts to hold in your mind. Doing so should, quite instantaneously, transform your perceptions of such circumstances and help you to relax and integrate. In this way, you're already assuming your loving purpose and potential, radiating light all over the place.

Start out with the understanding of why people think and act as they do, for example, due to their upbringing, social conditioning, or entrenchment within the system.

Choose one of the following concepts to become, assume, or live by during the day. Make it your aim to *be* these things. Choose another the next day to find the best one for you.

~ love

~ compassion

~ tolerance

~ transcendence (moving beyond situations without being emotionally triggered)

~ calmness

~ kindness

~ detachment (This doesn't mean you don't care. Instead, you're releasing emotional attachment to difficult situations and outcomes.)

~ peacekeeper (while being the peaceful one)

~ listener

~ creator

If you feel unpleasant emotions arise, return to focusing on *being* your concept of the day.

Remember, in being or becoming these positive things, you're not becoming a pushover or allowing anyone to walk all over you. You should still retain healthy boundaries that you can defend calmly and peacefully by taking mindful action. Once you get home, counsel yourself through any unpleasant emotions you experienced during the day. Remember to use acceptance, understanding, and forgiveness for yourself and others.

So, we've traversed the stages of awakening, considered ways of relating to family and friends, and reflected on the process of returning to the world as a spiritual being. What's next? You'd probably agree if I said your level of consciousness has been rising, right? So why stop there? There are multitudes of dimensions ahead of you to explore.

~

Chapter 6

Energies and Psychic Senses

As you progress through the awakening process, new potent possibilities come to light. Moving forward, as well as discussing the experiences you might be having, and providing means to manage the process and maintain your well-being, I'll weave in more tips and practices to enhance your continued journey.

It might seem like a deception that everything in the world seems so tangible and material, that when you look in the mirror, you see a physical body rather than a being of light or energy. Things are not what they appear to be. Why does life present itself as something other than it is? Rather than a deception, perhaps it's a challenge or question set by your higher self: Can you see the truth?

Once we realize the metaphysical nature of reality and our true energetic form, we can no longer ignore our innate abilities or remain passive to energies that influence us.

Kundalini and Energy Sensitivity

In Hinduism and yogic theory, Kundalini describes life-force energy lying dormant at the base of the spine. Often represented as a coiled serpent, once activated, it rises up through each of your main chakra energy centers. As it does so, kundalini awakening, or transformation, occurs, accompanied by often startling physical and emotional symptoms.

Kundalini awakening has very much to do with energetic movement and changes in consciousness. Its activation tends to accompany a shift in mind-set or rebirth, and in turn, transforms consciousness further. Your mind and body are one; hence, the expansion of awareness can result in physical eruptions of energy. Should you suddenly experience distinct symptoms such as fierce bodily heat, sweating, uncontrollable movements, restlessness, sleeplessness, or tingling, fizzling energy rising through the body or spine, it might be kundalini. Each of your chakras are being energetically stimulated and cleansed. This process is very much a purging or upgrade of consciousness; therefore, any underlying emotional difficulties you usually experience may become exacerbated and all the more apparent as they surface for healing. Your psychic senses, too, might feel uncomfortably open and receptive, receiving all sorts of thoughts and feelings from others.

I experienced kundalini early on in my awakening. I was sitting on the floor, meditating, and for the first time, I began to lose my sense of 'I', becoming almost nothing, yet everything all at once. My focus was no longer within my mind and body, but somewhere out there, or perhaps everywhere. It felt as if the top of my head was attached to an elastic band stretching off into the universe. Momentarily, part of my attention snapped back to my body as a sensation of heat began to form at the base of my spine. It was a warm, tingling, fizzling sensation, a bit like the sound of white noise but as a feeling. It rose slowly through my body, slightly more focused toward my back, and grew hotter and hotter. I was unable to move at all. Then, and this is unusual for kundalini, it seemed as if energy was also pouring *in* through the top of my head, creating a warm, loving feeling moving downward. I was alarmed, but there was nothing I could do except ride it out. In those two or three minutes, I experienced what seemed like infinity presenting itself as multicolored light within my mind. It was beautiful, blissful, yet overwhelming. I began to sweat. The lower sensation rose up until it reached the top of my head, overcoming the energy entering from above. Then, it was like someone turned out the lights, and it was over.

I went to bed after that because I didn't feel very well. But the next day, I became aware of intense anxiety. I had always suffered from moderate general and social anxiety, but that morning, I could barely function; I was anxious about absolutely everything. It was like kundalini brought my fear and dread to the surface and was rubbing it in my face. It took three weeks for the anxiety to subside, but after that, most significantly, I felt much better than ever before.

You can try to initiate kundalini through yogic exercises and guided meditations but prepare for a potentially challenging time. Everyone is different, of course, and some experience only a blissful, love-filled aftermath. If you haven't had a kundalini experience yet, don't worry. You may not require a sudden shift in energies and perceptions, and you're likely ascending and progressing quite nicely as you are. If you do have a kundalini experience of the challenging kind, then give yourself time to integrate it. Perform extensive self-care and relaxation, but try not to resist what kundalini is attempting to teach you. I faced my anxieties and worked through them, and found this accelerated the healing process. I encouraged and reassured myself through interactions, tasks, and leaving the house. Try not to push yourself excessively and seek emotional support if you need it.

Sensing Energies

During awakening, you might become more sensitive to psychic, astrological, lunar or solar energies, as well as electromagnetic fields, earthly locations, objects, and foodstuffs. All kinds of things give off energy for us to sense, and some significantly impact our well-being, both positively and negatively.

Many people suffer symptoms, such as dizziness, nausea, and fatigue, which they believe is due to the electromagnetic fields produced by electrical and communications equipment. Therefore, they attempt to reduce their exposure to them. You can protect against electromagnetic radiation by switching off your Wi-Fi at night or at other times when it's not in use, and by changing from a wireless home phone to a landline. Consider turning your mobile phone and tablets off as well, especially when you go to sleep. Many people sleep with their devices, still sending and receiving from the network, switched on, right beside their head. Since you are an electromagnetic being, consider reviewing your exposure to such energies, especially if you feel they affect you.

Our energetic reality seems to work on an algorithm, producing cycles of experience with variations. Hence, it makes sense why lunar and other astrological cycles affect people in certain ways. Creation wants us to experience all kinds of circumstances, and these tend to repeat, although slightly differently each time. Therefore, with astrology, we can predict, to a reasonable degree, what energies are coming up.

Reality, Creation, or the unified field is one infinite sea of energy, which means that energy is all that there is. Therefore, you are interpreting and experiencing energy all the time. Yet, as we fine-tune our inner senses, we learn to interpret information accurately that our five human senses cannot detect. Have you ever walked up to an ancient monument and felt its presence profoundly? What about when you walk into a house or venue and like or dislike the atmosphere? Your energy sensitivity becomes apparent as you gain perspective through the feeling of just knowing (claircognizance).

When I moved into my home, the energies were thick and very apparent. My house was built in 1890, so it had plenty of time to accumulate energies from its various inhabitants. It was like I was traveling through time. Whenever I walked into the kitchen, it overwhelmingly felt like I was stepping into the 1980s. Then, I had a lintel replaced above the kitchen window, and as the builders removed the old one, they pulled out a stash of newspapers all dated 1986. Whenever I walked into my bedroom, it felt like the 1960s. Wonderful confirmation arrived when I removed three layers of wallpaper, revealing a handwritten message on the wall from Jayne, age 14, 1962. I'm not sure why each room felt like a different time period, but, after a few weeks, they all began to feel like today, as we overwrote them with our energies.

It's Not Your Imagination

Our connection to plants, animals, and landscapes strengthens as we begin to sense and feel the essence and vibrancy of the natural world and immerse ourselves in its energies. For many, this is one of the most enjoyable developments of awakening. The aliveness and vividness of nature activates us so profoundly that mystical and transcendental experiences can be initiated. It can be hard to tear ourselves away and return to the city. It's not just because nature is pretty. There is scientific proof for our increased sense of well-being in nature. In the *Journal of Inflammation Research*, James L. Oschman, et al., note: 'Multi-disciplinary research has revealed that electrically conductive contact of the human body with the surface of the Earth (grounding or earthing) produces intriguing effects on physiology and health. Such effects relate to inflammation, immune responses, wound healing, and prevention and treatment of chronic inflammatory and autoimmune diseases.'[8]

Is this a well-kept secret? If there's not much profit in it, then probably so. Last time I checked, it costs nothing to take your shoes and socks off and stand on some grass. As a species, we have insulated ourselves with plastic and rubber soles from the Earth from which we arose. We realize there is indeed energy transfer between us and the Earth, which actively heals, and that for our health and well-being, we must connect with it (for about 20 minutes per day). Researchers have found that, through grounding (making contact with the earth), we receive negative ions that neutralize damaging free radicals that build up within our bodies. Negative ions are also present in the air, near moving water, and are more abundant in nature in general. You're not imagining things when you sense the fresh vibrancy of the life-force energy in nature.

When You Just Know the Energies Aren't Right

Sometimes you just know a substance isn't good for you. Have you ever experienced that? Even if logic tells you it's fine?

> *'I bought a snack pot at lunchtime, and the picture on the packaging looked really healthy. But as I held it, it didn't feel right, like it was negative or bad for me. I carried on, opened it, and tucked in. Although it was delicious, a short while later I began to feel dizzy, drowsy, and headachy. I wish I had trusted my instincts, because when I read the packaging, I saw that it had monosodium glutamate in it. I had suspected in the past that I'm sensitive to it, but this confirmed it. From now on, I'll read the packaging.'*

All substances emit energies, and even if you're not consciously paying attention, a subconscious niggle or 'no' can arise. As you become more open and receptive to energies, you can employ this skill regularly in deciding what to put in your body. Perhaps you have had an experience like the one with the snack pot, where the vibration of the substance felt too low to be good for you, and you were proven right. I urge you, therefore, to trust your intuition when sensing energies. It's usually the first of your innate inner senses to emerge and provides evidence of your abilities.

Intuitive and Psychic Development

I discussed earlier how our psychic and intuitive abilities tend to develop during awakening, the significance of this, and some phenomena that might spontaneously occur. So let's dive right into harnessing and using these skills.

Intuition is useful for:

⊚ gauging what an outcome will be

⊚ knowing if something is going well

⊚ knowing when something is or isn't right

⊚ making a choice or decision

⊚ discerning if someone is trustworthy or if they're hiding something

⊚ knowing if someone is in trouble (or other understandings about them even if they are not present)

> *For decades, I have seen ESP [extrasensory perception]
> occur in the laboratory on a day-to-day basis. As a physicist,
> I don't have to believe in this phenomenon any more than
> I have to believe in the existence of lasers – with which
> I have also worked extensively. Psychic abilities exist,
> just as lasers do, as has been repeatedly demonstrated
> by hundreds of experimental research studies.*
>
> RUSSELL TARG, PHYSICIST

Think for a moment how else you use your intuition. There are probably many ways in which you use it. Intuition is the psychic sense most frequently used in daily life. The word *psychic* is an umbrella term covering numerous different techniques for communicating or receiving information.

You can use your psychic abilities to (among other things):

- perceive the future (precognition) for yourself or others

- perceive others' thoughts (classic psychic reading or telepathy)

- receive information from atmospheres, places, or objects

- see or visit faraway places (remote viewing or astral projection)

- communicate with spirit guides, your higher self, loved ones who have passed over, or other spirits and beings (mediumship and channeling)

- read the Akashic records (the energetic record of everything that has occurred or ever will occur)

- perceive auras or energy blockages

- heal

You are capable of developing such skills given time, patience, and the right approach. You might excel at or favor one or two of them that can be used in everyday life. Seeing as these abilities are innately yours, and you, after all, are essentially spirit, you might as well nurture these skills on your way to realizing your infinite potential.

The Best Approach and State of Mind

Awakening enables us to identify less with our human self, or ego, and our earthly situation, and more with our higher self. So in approaching your intuitive and psychic development, take this standpoint: You can't go wrong. Imagine you *are* what you truly are – energetic soul consciousness. It's also best to approach such work with an attitude of playful enjoyment because, in this higher vibration, you better align with your higher self, higher dimensions of reality, and any earthly troubles melt into the background.

Blockers to intuitive and psychic senses include:

- pinning your hopes on results (generating resistance to failure)

- questioning the process (Is it working yet? Why isn't it working? What am I doing wrong? Instead, relax and let go.)

- choosing or deciding (instead, allow information to flow into your mind)

◉ overconcentration (instead, relax)

◉ tiredness, stress, and unpleasant emotions (creating a clouded mind and a low vibration)

You see, the absolute best way to get your inner senses flowing is to relax and let go. When we relax, our subconscious mind comes through, and our conscious (very human) mind fades away. As I said earlier, our subconscious mind is the bridge to the soul, allowing us to interface with higher aspects of self. Therefore, it's beneficial to take time to relax or meditate for at least 15 minutes before intentionally practicing psychic or intuitive skills (like using the pendulum or automatic writing) so that your subconscious has time to surface. I like to use meditation music to attune my vibration before such work.

I highly recommend daily meditation. Meditation trains our psyche into a calm and relaxed normal, in which our minds are less cluttered with thoughts and unpleasant emotions. Once we get the hang of it, we begin to exist closer to a state of bliss. A simple meditation where you listen to and feel your breathing is sufficient. In achieving a calmer state of consciousness, anything we receive psychically is more obviously originating from elsewhere and not from our human thoughts. We learn to tell the difference between our thoughts and what we are receiving. We know ourselves; therefore, anything else is a contrast. Our mind is quieter, ready for receiving, and our vibration is attuned.

Intuition is about feeling and just knowing. Although logic is great, during this process you're not weighing the pros and cons, thinking things through, or making decisions based on what you *should* do.

Listen for your inner reaction. The inner prompting that you get, yes or no, is the act of intuition. It may come to you as a feeling, a thought, or you may even hear a voice saying, 'No!' How your inner self will speak to you is something that you have to discover for yourself, but the response will come.

HENRY REED, PH.D.

Following are a few examples of when your intuition is coming through:

- You just know that everything will be okay.

- You have a feeling that a person will become a good friend.

- You have the urge or feel the pull to take a particular path in life.

- You experience a sense of dread or feel excited (because you're sensing a potential future).

The 'just knowing' or 'feeling like' are key to intuition, and you can learn to trust these by writing down your intuitions as they arise and seeing what the outcomes are. In this way, you're better able to stick to your optimal life path. Your higher self knows your most beneficial path in life, and as intuition comes from higher aspects of self, you can navigate life in the most meaningful and enjoyable way. Yes, challenges still arise, but by using your intuition, you can overcome them more easily.

To know or recognize if you are using your psychic senses, we need to explore the all-important clairs. These are clairvoyance, clairaudience, claircognizance, and clairsentience, and I discuss these next. But first, use the following pendulum exercise to get your intuition flowing.

🦋 EXERCISE: PENDULUM PRACTICE 🦋

The pendulum is a crystal, or a piece of metal or wood suspended from a chain or piece of string, and swung. Although it's a handy tool for divination, you can also use it to enhance your intuition.

Many a doubter will say that you're merely swinging the pendulum yourself, when in fact you are completely detached from the whole process, allowing the pendulum to swing on its own. But it's not *really* swinging on its own. By relaxing and letting your subconscious mind take control, you allow the answers to your questions to arise from deep within. Your subconscious provides answers by causing micro-movements in your arm muscles without your conscious awareness. After all, intuition arrives subconsciously, and the pendulum only makes your intuitive senses more apparent. If you don't have a pendulum, you can make one by tying to a string a regularly shaped object of a decent weight, or you can use a long necklace with a suitably heavy pendant.

1. Think of some questions to ask your intuition that require yes or no answers.

2. Take 15 minutes to relax or meditate.

3. Pinch the top of the string between your forefinger and thumb.

4. Hold your arm out, not too rigidly but slightly bent.

5. Give the pendulum a test swing and sense or feel it as if you are one with it. Become the pendulum as it becomes part of you. Neither try nor not try to swing it. Allow your arm simply to be.

6. Find out what the 'yes,' 'no,' and 'not sure' answers will be. 'Yes' and 'no' are usually represented by either forward and backward, or left and right swings. 'Not sure' is a circular motion or no movement at all.

7. Completely detach yourself from the responses. Looking away from the pendulum for a few moments can help.

8. Say, 'Show me yes,' and wait nonjudgmentally for a swing. You might receive only tiny swings at first. Make a note of which type you receive.

9. Say, 'Show me no,' and make a note of the swing.

10. Say, 'Show me not sure,' and make a note. Sometimes, 'not sure' also means that you are not supposed to receive such knowledge at this time.

11. Remaining relaxed, go ahead and ask your questions, taking your time. Remain detached, as if your arm is not yours at the moment.

You can pause between questions to write down your insights.

It can take several sessions for your subconscious mind to get into the swing of using your pendulum. Try to have patience and approach this practice with playful enjoyment, pinning no hopes on the outcome. Over time, more pronounced swings will develop, and you can move on to using this tool for communicating with your higher self or spirit guides if you wish. Set the intention to tune in to them, in love and light and for your highest good, and proceed to ask them questions.

The Clairs

Your third eye is the receiver of the clairs, those subtle psychic senses that augment our reality, often without us being aware we're using them. When people begin to practice their clairs, they ask, 'How do I know I'm not making it all up or imagining things?' And that's a good question. Psychics, mediums, and channelers all use one or more of their clairs when tuning in to information or communication. Over time, they learn to discern the difference between their own thoughts and the information they receive. They recognize their clairs, and you can too. Pay attention to the following:

- What the context is, for example, you've just opened up for communication or asked a question of spirit.

- How the process feels, for example, the information can feel clearer, more precise, and highly significant.

- The way the clairs just 'pop in there' or arrive as if from nowhere, with no trail of thought leading to them.

- The way they contrast against the backdrop of a calm, meditative mind, achieved through meditation.

'The energies are favorable for psychic communication today. Three times my daughter has said what I was thinking before I had a chance to say it. And I keep reading my husband's mind, too, because he keeps saying, "I was just about to say that!"'

Psychic skills are very subtle. There won't be a big signpost that pops up to say, 'You're doing it now.' The four clairs can be mistaken for your own thought or imagination, and that's why we spend most of our lives unaware of them, brushing off seemingly psychic events as coincidences or saying, 'That was weird.' You have probably been using your clairs all your life but never recognized them.

Clairvoyance

Clairvoyance happens in the mind's eye in the same way as you'd picture something, experience a memory, or have a daydream. The difference is that clairvoyant images or visions tend to arrive in your mind as if they've been put there. If you are very relaxed, clairvoyance can be more vivid and colorful than imagination or memory recall, and becomes completely immersive; this happens during astral projection and past-life regression. Those with aphantasia are generally unable to use clairvoyance, although one of the other clairs is usually enhanced to compensate.

Claircognizance

Intuition is, in effect, claircognizance coming from within. Yet when we mention claircognizance, we're usually referring to the receiving of wisdom and knowledge from distinct sources, such as spirit or the Akashic records. It's just knowing something, even if it contradicts logic or available information. When you ask for guidance from your higher self, the response often arrives as an innate knowledge of the answer. When using the tarot, you just know how the individual cards contribute to the meaning of the entire spread relevant to the person you are reading for. We can also instinctively know how to perform a task, such as fix a bike or navigate to a destination, by claircognizantly receiving the information from the fabric of Creation or from the collective consciousness.

Engineer and inventor Nikola Tesla has been credited with saying, *'My brain is only a receiver, in the universe there is a core from which we obtain knowledge, strength, and inspiration, I have not penetrated into the secrets of this core, but I know that it exists.'* Tesla had a clear and strong connection with a universal intelligence with which we, too, can foster an affinity. Perhaps he acquired some of his groundbreaking technical knowledge from this universal 'core' in which higher knowledge is abundant. He aimed to provide infinite free energy for all, and it's said that others stole and suppressed his inventions for their own profit. Perhaps certain truths are destined to emerge within this reality from some higher realm through individuals' claircognizant knowing.

Clairsentience

Feeling and sensation come into play here as you experience emotion from external sources as if it is your own. You may also feel the pain or discomfort of others within your body as if mirroring their experiences. It is very much like virtual empathy, where you feel what it is like to be someone else. Spirit guides can communicate via clairsentience, and this manifests in the powerful feeling of love you might receive when you connect with them. You might also receive emotions and physical feelings from loved ones, beloved pets, or strangers. Even if you're not feeling one way or another, when they come near to you, you suddenly share in their emotions. Empaths are – usually involuntarily – using clairsentience when they experience others' emotions.

Clairaudience

We experience clairaudience as a voice, voices, or sounds. Not heard with our ears, the sounds are perceived within the mind, similar to our internal monologue – that voice we use to talk to ourselves in our head. Researchers have discovered that not everyone has an inner monologue, a similar situation to aphantasia, so these individuals, whose minds are perfectly normal, seeing as we are each unique, may never experience clairaudience. Clairaudience usually occurs during spirit communication, so psychic mediums often pick it up. If you do have it, you might make an excellent medium yourself! It also sometimes happens when psychically receiving the thoughts of other human beings.

I first noticed I was clairaudient when, as I was going to sleep at night, I would hear all sorts of voices within my mind. I'm sure many would think this a good reason for a mental health evaluation, but it only occurred when I was very relaxed and on the verge of sleep, hence my subconscious mind was dominant. The voices would phase in and out, were both male and female, sometimes numerous, and would occasionally speak in different languages! They were just talking about random things. It was rather annoying when one would shout out and jolt me from my doze. By listening to them, I surmised that I was picking up on spirits somewhere around, perhaps earthbound ones, and I didn't really want that. So I set the intention to close the doors of communication in my mind and open them only when I chose. The voices stopped. From a spiritual protection and boundary-setting perspective, it's vital to remember that your free will is paramount. If you're receiving unwanted communication, you can close your mind by merely deciding to do so. It is *your* mind, after all.

Spiritual awakening helps many individuals to realize their intuitive and psychic abilities and to use them in helpful ways. One method is mind-to-mind communication, which enables us to understand and support others better. We are not reading their thoughts by poking around in their heads, but are, instead, sharing more deeply all that they are already willing to share.

🦋 Exercise: Using Psychic Skills 🦋 to Help Someone

Next time you're having a conversation with a loved one or friend, pay attention to your inner senses. You may already visualize what others describe or naturally empathize with them anyway. But, in performing this practice, you can gain greater awareness of the abilities you're already using, fine-tune them to gain more insight, and have even greater understanding of others to assist them better. You don't have to tell them you are practicing your psychic abilities, because this is an exercise in attentively listening. You are simply using *more* of your senses. Of course, let them know about your practice if you wish.

1. As the conversation begins, be mindful of relaxing, being open, and holding love in your heart.

2. Give the person your full attention, and while listening to their words, imagine you are one with them, as if you are *becoming* them.

3. If you wish, you can visualize your energy field expanding and including them. Our individual electromagnetic fields frequently intersect other people's, so this is nothing new.

4. Notice your emotions. How do you feel? For validation, ask them how they feel and see if it matches.

5. Next, become aware of any mental images arriving in your mind. You may be picturing along with their descriptions, but do any images appear in your mind's eye *before* they speak? For example, you see a coffee cup, and then

your friend tells you she went for coffee with her sister yesterday.

6. Now, become aware of your sense of knowing. Before the person finishes their story or description, what do you just know they will say? Then wait and see. What additional unsaid knowing do you receive about their experiences? If you wish, you can ask them to elaborate on certain things in order to validate your perceptions.

Practice is required, but over time, through experience, you'll learn how to discern your own thoughts and emotions from those you are receiving. If you are already psychically or empathically sensitive, you might be thinking: What if I don't want to experience more of the thoughts and feelings of others? You may be feeling this way because you are not shielding yourself well enough, are overly open and receptive (like when I was receiving unwanted clairaudience), or because the whole process is happening in an unfettered and unstructured way. This leads us to spiritual protection.

Spiritual Protection

Just as we secure our home at night, or try not to provoke angry or aggressive people, we take measures to protect ourselves from unwanted spirit encounters and unpleasant energies. Spiritual protection is useful not only during intuitive and psychic practice but also for life in general. Other planes and dimensions of existence are not *all* love and light, as negative polarity exists throughout the universe. I'm not trying to scare anyone, quite the opposite. I offer simple tools most beneficial for feeling safe and protected, no matter who or what you intentionally or unintentionally connect with and regardless of where you send your consciousness. If you astral project into another galaxy, you don't want to travel with the belief that you might come across malevolent beings, because that is what you'll attract. If you're negatively affected by lunar or other astrological energies, you may want to shield yourself. Should you be experiencing empathic interference, you might require your own energetic protection.

Your Attitude Protects You

Your reality manifests according to your thoughts, beliefs, and vibration. You can, therefore, freely define who or what you permit within your reality or personal space. You manifest the whole show.

With this attitude, you claim your sovereignty and release any feelings of vulnerability, which only serve to manifest more circumstances in which to feel vulnerable. Stand firm in your power and take charge of your energies. If you believe that the cycles of the moon significantly affect you, then they will. 'But they do!' many will say. That's because many people *allow* the moon, Mercury, Venus, or other planetary bodies to have excessive influence over their energies and emotions. It's the same for thought-forms, earthbound spirits, and spirit attachments (spirits that hang around a certain person). If we adopt the mind-set that 'I have a spirit following me around and it won't go away,' then it won't. You are effectively permitting it to stay. You want it to go away, but are incredibly frustrated that it won't, thinking it won't, so it doesn't. 'It's gone!' is a more effective attitude, in conjunction with other steps like the cleansing with smoke technique in Chapter 3 (*see p.86*).

The attitude of 'This is my reality, and I am in charge of it,' will provide extensive protection for you, your energies, home, and loved ones. If you think about it, thought-forms and spirits are not of this reality. Are they? You are the one who has incarnated here, with an earthly physical body with the power to co-create. They haven't. So, in believing you are powerless, that is what you'll be. Realize that the earthly realm is *your* reality, during your human lifetime anyway. Therefore, you have far more power than beings who don't even have the right body to be here. You can take the approach that you are an infinite, immortal, energetic being (with the right earthly body), untouchable or invincible within your powerful energy.

Your Intention

In addition to your confident, empowered attitude, you can consciously speak your intention to create protection. Words are magical tools to manifest reality. So, if you require protection from psychically received emotions, thoughts, or unpleasant energies, you can recite the following to yourself any time you wish.

- ⊚ 'I am safe and protected at all times.'

- ⊚ 'My energy field is sacred and secure.'

- ⊚ 'I am divinely guided and protected.'

- 'I am confident in my powerful energies.'

- 'My family and I are fully protected.'

- 'My home is a sacred space of positive energies.'

Another protection technique involving intention is challenging the spirits or other beings that you might encounter during spirit communication, channeling, or journeying. The process involves challenging them in the name of a positive symbol or concept that you hold most sacred. You can challenge them in the name of love and light, God, Creation, an archangel, your ancestors, or any other high vibrational concept you wish. For example, 'I challenge you with the highest intentions, for the greatest good, in the name of Christ's consciousness.' This statement effectively creates a wall of light through which nothing of a low vibration may pass.

Vibrational Protection

I've never met anyone who can maintain a high vibration *all* the time. It's rare for a human lifetime to be a consistently blissful experience, even if you have transcended all earthly illusions and found inner peace. Sometimes, life throws you a curveball to bat or dodge. But in having the intention to heal, reflect, experience, and grow, you're working toward a higher, happier, loving vibration. Such a focus is more than enough to repel any unwanted energies.

In working toward a higher vibration, the highest of which is love, we move out of alignment with darker or unhelpful energies. Your brilliant light illuminates the darkness. Negatively polarized beings feed on fear, but love has the potential to turn them positive, and they don't want that, so they leave you alone. They also know they can't influence you, so they don't bother. In Chapters 7 and 8, I'll guide you through ways to raise your vibration.

Empathic Protection

Empaths are often engulfed in and overcome by others' unpleasant-feeling emotions. It's lovely to share in the joy of a group, but when every other person you come across is having a bad day, yours takes a dark turn too. As an empath, I've found the best way to protect myself from empathic interference is to visualize the emotions of others as a cloud around me. Then, using my mind's eye, I see the cloud moving away, going 'over there,' separate from me. I can still observe it and help others if they're feeling down because, with empathy, we can truly understand what others are going through. But I'm no longer lost in the cloud of emotions. In addition, through regular meditation practice, I've grown to know myself better; therefore, when I pick up on people's emotions, I know which ones belong to me and which ones to separate out.

Practical Methods for Protection

Crystals

You can use crystals for protection, and many swear by their effectiveness. Tried and tested over time, their crystalline structures either absorb, transmute, or shield us from unpleasant energies. Such stones also instill a sense of strength and safety, so that you manifest more of the same. You can put crystals in your pockets or bag, place them on your desk, or around rooms. When using crystals for protection, program them with the intention to protect you.

Amethyst, with its high vibration, is a transmuter of negative energies. It inspires peace, calmness, acceptance, and forgiveness, and fosters a greater connection with the divine.

Black obsidian is a beloved shamanic stone, a shielder and absorber of other's destructive intentions and unpleasant emotions. Many also use it to safeguard against the electro-magnetic fields produced by electrical devices.

Black tourmaline is a great all-rounder. A transmuter of energies from negative into positive, it also repels and shields.

Fluorite, a psychic protection stone, enhances your energy field, strengthening your vital energies. It is said to render your energy field invisible should you wish to become so for a while.

Hematite is a shielding and protecting stone that helps you maintain your energetic boundaries.

Labradorite protects against psychic attack and anyone who might be focusing upon you.

Raising the Vibration of Your Home

I recommend cleaning your home and giving away anything that reminds you of any unhappier times. Open the windows because this also clears a great deal of stagnant energy. As per the ancient Chinese art of Feng Shui, which you can study in detail, intuitively position objects and furniture in such a way as to enhance energy flow around your home. See what feels right through trial and error.

Salt, which has a crystalline structure, is terrific for the absorption of unwanted energies. Sprinkle salt along the edges of your rooms and the windowsills. Leave it for 24 hours, sweep or vacuum it up, and empty it outside in the garbage.

Pleasant items like flowers, drawings, cushions, and cloth inspire a high vibration, adding to your psychic protection. I'm not recommending you go out and spend lots of money on stuff, but when you choose an item, pause and reflect on how it makes you feel. Does it raise your vibration? Often, pre-loved secondhand items have a high vibrational history and feel less blank and clinical than something newly manufactured. When you bring new items home you can also cleanse them with smoke to reset their energies.

I like to burn incense once a day to remove any unpleasant energies that may have accumulated. Rose and lavender, my personal favorites, are of a particularly high vibration.

Music

Have you ever noticed how music changes the vibration in a room? Everyone can be hanging around, lost in thought or focusing intently on some social media influence, then someone puts on a song, and everyone livens up, starts chatting or bopping along. If music makes you feel good, then it's of a high vibration. Some music, as you might observe, makes you feel sad or melancholy, and although this helps to purge unpleasant emotion, which you can work with to heal, it obviously won't raise your vibration at that moment. So you can use pleasant music to change the ambient vibration, which your own vibration entrains and naturally acts as protection. Singing bowls, tingsha bells, tuning forks, and meditation music have the same effect.

The Feline Factor

I recommend cats. This might sound like the advice of a crazy cat lady (and if you're thinking that about me, you might be right), but kidding aside, I recommend them to anyone who has the inclination, time, and commitment to providing one with a loving home. I have two. Although many beloved pets, such as dogs, have wonderfully high vibrations and healing effects, cats are perceived by many as being powerful guardians who ward off unwanted energetic influences. They can tune in to energy fields, alternate dimensions, and portals that we may overlook. If your cat avoids certain areas of your home, those corners, nooks, and crannies may require some energetic cleansing.

Remember, your thoughts, beliefs, and vibration manifest your reality. The following process uses visualization and intention to create robust protection.

🦋 Exercise: Protective Light Practice 🦋

You can create protective golden-white light to armor yourself or your home and set it there to stay. All negative energies will remain outside of this field, and you can happily and confidently carry on with your day. This process involves visualization; if this is tricky for you, then intuit or feel your creation.

1. Close your eyes and take three slow rhythmic deep breaths into your belly. With each breath, notice yourself relaxing more.

2. Take the attitude of being a powerful, loving, spiritual being.

3. Set the intention to form an impenetrable bubble of high vibrational protection around you.

4. Visualize brilliant whitish, golden light gathering from the very fabric of Creation and forming a sphere around your body from head to toe.

5. In your mind's eye, sense or see the sphere becoming thicker and brighter.

6. Set it there to stay by directing a thought of permanence toward it.

7. Take one more deep breath in and out, safe in the knowledge you are fully protected.

8. Open your eyes when you're ready.

Chapter 7

Practices for Spiritual Growth

Like the chrysalis cracking open and a butterfly emerging, you, too, might be ready to take flight. The following concepts can help you to do just that.

Third-Eye Activation

> *The light of the body is the eye: if therefore thine eye be single, thy whole body shall be full of light.*
>
> MATTHEW 6:22

Does the Bible give us a clue about the existence of the third eye? Many interpret the Bible in esoteric and metaphysical ways. We have sight, hearing, smell, taste, and touch, but many have discovered their sixth sense, received by their third eye, allowing them to peer into spiritual dimensions. That which is usually unseen or undetectable is highly perceptible if we use our innate sixth sense. The third eye is the receiver of the clairs; it not only sees but also knows and hears. Ordinarily, our five senses are our receivers of information, and we transmit (or communicate) through speech and actions. But many are unaware that we also communicate energetically via thought, vibration, emotion, and intention, and the third eye is the receiver of such energies. Also known as the *Ajna* chakra, the third eye is the gateway to inpourings of light and wisdom from the very fabric of Creation; hence 'thy whole body shall be full of light' when you use your 'single' eye. Then there's time perception, time being a linear phenomenon from our human point of view, yet it holds no sway over the third eye's limitless perceptual capabilities. Hence, we *can* perceive possible futures and intuitively make the best choices.

So why open your third eye? Well, if you'd like to use it to perceive beyond the veil of the physical, why not? Not using it is like having two legs but never figuring out, or being shown, how to walk. The third eye has limitless potential and is overlooked by most people who don't even know it exists, with no clue how to use it. The funny thing is, most of us do use it to some degree. You might have heard of techniques to help you to open your third eye, but you mustn't assume it was ever closed in the first place. It doesn't exactly have eyelids. It just needs a bit of cleansing, exercise, and intentional practice.

Your *Ajna* chakra, like all your chakras, is an energy center, and therefore greatly affected by your thoughts, perceptions, and vibration. Each chakra is thus adjusted, in part, by personality balancing, understanding yourself, and inner healing. We can identify blockages or where something seems to be out of balance in ours or others' chakras. For example, if you struggle to understand and accept yourself, your sacral chakra may require some healing. If a workmate has an unruly, unregulated ego, then their solar plexus chakra may be suffering from blockage. If a family member talks a lot without listening, their throat chakra might require some conscious attention. Our chakras reflect imbalances within ourselves, and should we become aware of such shadow aspects and choose to heal them, our chakras naturally adjust. The third eye chakra is traditionally associated with intuition, vision, and wisdom. If you wish to enhance its use, the best way is to exercise it:

- Practice your intuition and psychic abilities (using the clairs).

- Connect with higher aspects of self during meditation, perhaps to receive wisdom and guidance.

- Contemplate the knowledge and foresight you receive. Contemplation is sitting quietly and mindfully, mulling over and digesting your realizations, then integrating them into your psyche, helping to balance your third eye chakra further.

- Practice energy mindfulness meditation, becoming a quiet point of awareness and sensing and observing nonjudgmentally the energies in the space around you. This is best done out in nature to psychically connect with the natural world and all its elements and beings.

As you activate your third eye, it's vital to do so with the highest intentions and for the greatest good. A person developing psychokinesis so they can poke people from a distance just to make them jump is not exactly acting in anyone's best interest. Some people do work on their third eye for such negative ends. These kinds of intentions tend to arise when people concentrate on cleansing and activating their third eye without attending to their other chakras. Imagine someone developing their third eye while their sacral, solar plexus, and heart chakras are blocked. That person might live with an undercurrent of anger and frustration, struggling to get on with other people, and generally lacking in love and compassion for themselves or others. Imagine what psychic mischief they'd be getting into as a result, conjuring up all sorts of thought-forms, and remote viewing where they shouldn't. I'm sure you'll agree that I can't suggest third-eye activation without recommending we sort out our other six chakras at the same time. It stands to reason that each of our chakras contributes to our overall energetic harmony. The following third-eye activation exercise includes all the chakras, so ensures positive outcomes. After this, I'll provide further practice for focusing only on your third eye.

❧ EXERCISE: CHAKRA ACTIVATION ❧

As with any exercise, it's best to read through the steps a few times so you won't need to refer back to them during meditation. It might look like a lot, but it becomes second nature through practice.

1. Sit on the floor or a chair. Straighten your back, with your vertebrae stacked one on top of the other so that energy can flow straight up your spine.

2. Close your eyes and focus on your breath for about 10 minutes. When thoughts arrive, allow them to float away gently with love.

3. Sense or visualize golden healing prana energy streaming up from the Earth, up your spine, and entering each chakra in turn. As it does so, allow your chakras to glow brightly, filling your inner vision with their corresponding colors. Notice each chakra spinning like a wheel, unblocking, cleansing, and activating.

4. Spend about two minutes on each chakra and, in addition to the energy cleansing, focus on the following concepts:

   ~ Root chakra (red) at the base of your spine. Allow any low vibratory emotions you may experience in life (such as anxiety, disappointment, or frustration) to calm.

   ~ Sacral chakra (orange) at your lower abdomen. Welcome self-acceptance. Be open to fully accepting everything about yourself as a unique, magnificent being.

   ~ Solar plexus chakra (yellow) at your upper abdomen. You intuitively realize your purpose now and who you are. Experience your infinite true self.

   ~ Heart chakra (green) at the center of your chest. Allow love to overcome you, love for yourself, everyone, and everything.

   ~ Throat chakra (blue) at your throat. Step into your truth and your ability to speak it. Commit to listening nonjudgmentally.

- Third eye chakra (indigo) between your eyebrows. Open up to your universal connection with inpourings of intelligent energy and wisdom. Your clairs are becoming vivid and distinct.

- Crown chakra (violet) just above the top of your head. Experience the oneness of all things as all your chakras align energetically in perfect harmony.

5. End the meditation when you're ready.

If you're satisfied with the brightness and radiance of each chakra, you can focus on third-eye activation only.

🦋 Exercise: Third-Eye Activation 🦋

1. Perform steps one and two from the previous exercise.

2. Bring your attention to the point between your eyebrows, as if looking at that space within your head. At the same time, hold the intention of creating openness and free-flowing clarity.

3. Focus on this point for about five minutes and open your eyes when you're ready.

The Pineal Gland

The physical manifestation of your third eye might also require attention. Otherwise, the work is only half done.

> *The pineal, whose function was intuitively recognized by ancient civilizations and, until recently, greatly underestimated by modern science, serves to assist us in bonding with the universe.*
>
> JACOB LIBERMAN, O.D., PH.D.

The pineal gland is wired to the visual cortex of the brain and contains water, rods, and cones (retinal tissue) similar to a normal eye, yet there is no light in the brain for it to receive. What, therefore, is it receiving, locked in the center of your brain? The pineal gland also contains tiny calcite crystals that generate an electrical charge, and consequently electromagnetic fields, which can potentially tune in to information. As Joe Dispenza says in his book *Becoming Supernatural*: 'The crystals in our pineal gland, acting like a cosmic antenna, are the doorway to these higher vibrational realms of light and information. This is how we have internal experiences that are more real than our external ones.'[9]

To allow ourselves optimal opportunities for growth and development, to be able to connect with the all, and to enhance our inner realizations, we can prioritize the health of our pineal gland. It tends to become calcified and hardened with residual material because it is especially vulnerable to toxins and chemicals that we ingest or come into contact with, impairing its functioning. A calcified pineal gland can also result in lowered melatonin production, affecting our sleep cycles and circadian rhythm. There are measures you can take on an ongoing basis to prevent its calcification.

Reduce fluoride exposure. If you live in an area where the water is fluoridated, consider switching to fluoride-free mineral water. Our kidneys need water to remove toxins and waste effectively, and for a plethora of other reasons, so don't be discouraged from drinking water. But it's best to find the purest source possible. The water where I live is not fluoridated, but it sure does smell of chlorine, so my family and I use a water distiller to purify it. We then remineralize it with a special mineral solution so that we know exactly what's in it. We also use fluoride-free toothpaste because fluoride is absorbed through your oral tissue and can eventually work its way to the pineal gland. I have dental fluorosis, white spots in my teeth due to overexposure to fluoride as a child. Although there is evidence that fluoride strengthens your teeth, in excessive amounts, the adverse effects on teeth have also been proven.

Our bodies need calcium for many essential functions. However, consider checking that any calcium supplements you ingest don't contain calcium carbonate. Chemical analysis of calcified pineal glands often shows the presence of calcium carbonate.[10] Corpora arenaceal or 'brain sand' refers to the calcified structures within the pineal gland. I always choose vitamin and mineral supplements from natural sources so that my family and I only ingest foods as nature intended. Try to avoid processed foods when possible, and go organic if you can, because many pesticides, additives, and preservatives contain fluoride and calcium compounds and other toxins that can potentially work their way into your pineal gland, impairing its functioning.

Certain foods act as detoxifiers of neurotoxins like fluoride, and some as chelators (removers) of heavy metals such as mercury. Many people have found the following foods and supplements beneficial for the pineal gland, since they enhance the use of their third eye (always read the recommended dosages):

- cilantro (or coriander)

- kelp

- chlorella

- spirulina

- wheatgrass

- beetroot

Higher-Self Communication

Who or what is your higher self? Your higher self is perhaps you in the far, distant, unimaginable future. The you that you will become after you have ascended to higher dimensions and raised your vibration to an inconceivably high level over aeons of 'time.'

Assuming that earthly reality is not the only plane, dimension, or frequency of existence, it's reasonable to suspect that higher beings might exist in these 'places.' You may have heard the term *ascension*, the upward progression through the layers of existence, lifetime after lifetime. We learn and evolve until we reach elevated states of lovingness and compassion, even enlightenment, on our way to perhaps angelic beingness, or becoming our higher self.

We might suspect that alternate realities have properties somewhat different from our own. For example, instead of having four dimensions (length, depth and height, plus time flowing in one direction), there are additional dimensions, say a fifth, where time also flows the other way. According to superstring theory, the universe has as many as ten dimensions, which are, of course, totally outside of our perceptual capabilities (currently). Perhaps beings inhabiting such places can move around in time at will, or from their perspective, time doesn't exist at all. Therefore, they exist outside of time. If time has no influence outside of our reality, perhaps future incarnations of us, our higher self or selves, exist simultaneously with us. Hence, we can communicate with them in real time.

Who wouldn't want to connect with a highly advanced version of themselves? Often, our higher self acts as a mirror reflecting our inner and outer worlds for us to see truly, illuminating our shadows and that which we've been overlooking. While immersed in our personal perceptions, we often fail to see the bigger picture.

Our higher self wants us to have our own experiences, so it doesn't tell us what to do. Instead, we receive gentle guidance where appropriate. It's also unlikely to give us future predictions, especially long-term ones, because the future is subject to change, especially the further ahead you look. Instead, it provides a little foresight of possible timelines just to help you stay on track. Our higher self guides our progression and efficient use of experiential catalysts while allowing us to make our own decisions. In this way, our free will remains intact. This higher being has an interest in doing all this because what our higher self is now, we will become; therefore, by assisting us – part of itself – it contributes to its own self-development.

You may wish to connect with your higher self to (among other things):

- receive guidance and foresight

- help in decision-making

- receive healing energy

- understand yourself better

- find sources of pain or other unpleasant emotions for healing

- receive knowledge and wisdom

- understand spiritual, metaphysical, and esoteric concepts better

- understand anything better

- realize your purpose

- review past lives

Do we share a higher self with others? Well, this is the premise for the 'twin flame' phenomenon and for 'split incarnations.' Again, due to the irrelevancy of time, your higher self, so highly advanced, can perhaps project incarnations into various times and places. All are essentially alternate versions of you, each with its own personality, circumstances, and life experiences. If you go up the tree a little further from your higher self, it, too, may have a higher self, all the way up to the source of Creation, where, at the highest level, everything merges with the all. Essentially then, we are all one person, one being, having infinite incarnations. We could get our minds in knots for days with such topics, but what fun it is to explore.

It's common to assume your higher self is separate from you, when in actuality, you *are* your higher self. It is possibly projecting you, via thought and intention, into this reality. Therefore, you can take the standpoint of your higher self when interpreting your experiences, by instead observing *as* infinite awareness, rather than limited physicality. As Alan Watts notes, *'So you got to... meditate in such a way that you identify with your higher self. How do you do that? Well, you start by watching all your thoughts. Very carefully. Watching your feelings, watching your emotions. So that you begin to build up a sense of separation between the watcher and what is watched.'*[11]

So you see, you become the impartial observer of all that happens, a point of awareness that *watches* the sights, sounds, thoughts, and emotions. Then you find that the observer is pure awareness, immaculate higher consciousness – perhaps the point of view of your higher self – itself.

Now, we can also communicate with our higher self as if it were a separate being, while still remembering that, although it is communicative, it is still part of you. Over time, using your clairs, you can learn to converse with your higher self. The connection feels a certain way that's hard to describe, but you'll subconsciously learn to recognize it through practice. It can feel like an upward pull, something higher, an angelic vibration, a lightness, and a loving purity, a beautiful being connecting with your own energies.

Self-hypnosis is an effective way to connect with your higher self and creates a highly immersive and compelling experience, brimming with inner visuals, claircognizant knowing, even sounds, emotions, and sensations.

🦋 Exercise: Higher-Self Communication 🦋 Technique

Self-hypnosis is a state of deep relaxation where your subconscious mind becomes dominant, allowing your conscious mind to rest. You won't 'go under,' and you know you are doing it simply by feeling very relaxed. You can stop at any time by opening your eyes. This process helps you become accustomed to 'tuning in' so that you can do it anytime. To avoid falling asleep, approach this exercise with definite intention and focused concentration while you're relaxing. Prepare three questions before you begin and commit them to memory. If you read the process through a couple of times, it'll become easy to remember because it's like a story.

1. Put on some relaxing meditation music and listen intently for approximately 15 minutes. If thoughts arrive, happily bring your attention back to the music. Notice yourself aligning to its pleasant vibration and feel yourself drifting deeper into relaxation.

2. Take three slow, deep breaths, breathing in relaxation and breathing out any stress and tension.

3. Take another five minutes to relax your entire body. Notice a sinking-down feeling at your feet, legs, lower body, upper body, arms, and especially your shoulders and facial muscles.

4. Visualize or sense yourself strolling through a beautiful garden in the sunshine. Become aware of the colors and details of the trees, plants, and flowers. Hear birds singing and feel a gentle breeze on your skin. Take time to paint this landscape within your mind.

5. Set the intention to meet your higher self and invite them into the garden. Say, either in your mind or out loud, 'I invite my higher self to join me in love and light.'

6. Notice your higher self in the distance, presenting as a being of light. Sense their vibrant, loving energies as they walk toward you.

7. Once they reach you, greet and thank them, and ask your first question.

8. Listen for their response. You may hear it as a voice, as a sense of just knowing the answer, as images overlaying the scene, or as pleasant emotion. Take your time.

9. Ask your two remaining questions in the same way.

10. Thank your higher self and observe them walking away into the garden, disappearing altogether.

11. Relax for a little longer and open your eyes when you're ready.

Past-Life Remembering and Karma

When we are born, we embark on a brand-new journey, having consciously forgotten previous ones. But do we forget completely? There are various documentaries and books about young children who seem to remember past lifetimes, describing their former parents, where they lived, their occupations, and even how they died. For many years, psychiatrist and professor Ian Stevenson researched the phenomenon of reincarnation in cases of children from around the world who seemed to recall previous lives. He set out to investigate such cases, often discovering surprising validation of the children's memories, skills carried over, and even repeating birthmarks and deformities. He studied around three thousand cases and wrote many books and papers on reincarnation. Of course, much of the scientific community criticized or ignored his work.

The Many Incarnations of Your Soul

Why should we be interested in our past lives? Sometimes we want to know about them out of curiosity, to understand ourselves better, or because we suspect a loved one in this life might have incarnated with us before. Previous lives may also have shaped, to some extent, who we are today and the experiences we are having.

You live in a version of society that others molded and shaped before you were born. Genetically, you are part of a continually evolving species. Yet, you are soul consciousness experiencing a piece of human evolution. Your journey didn't begin in this lifetime nor will it end here.

Reincarnation, at least as I conceive it, does not nullify what we know about evolution and genetics. It suggests, however, that there may be two streams of evolution – the biological one and a personal one – and that during terrestrial lives these streams may interact.

IAN STEVENSON, M.D.

Our previous lifetimes, although complete from our point of view, may not be done and dusted; and in fact, may be a continuous journey of personal evolution. Sometimes, there can be residual attachments, emotions, regrets, resentments, or even longing from past lives, just out of conscious reach, within our subconscious mind, still affecting us today.

The Ever-Turning Wheel of Karma

Then there's karma, a concept in Hinduism and Buddhism. It arises from our intentions and actions, during this life and others, influencing our experiences today. Karma is not a punishment or reward; it's more like cause and effect. Our higher self wants us to learn, experience, grow, and evolve, as per the nature of Creation itself. To do this, we must experience both sides of the coin, what everything is like from the perspective of the one dishing out the actions and the one on the receiving end, even if both are yourself. In one lifetime, you might be a hardened business owner, paying your employees a meager wage, and in the next life, you might have to toil night and day for very little pay. You may also experience a lifetime of freedom, abundance, and bliss, caring little for others, then in the next, endure restrictive circumstances, depending on others for survival.

> *'My past-life reading taught me a few things about myself. It was 1930, and I was a young man of 22, smartly dressed, living on the East Coast in the U.S. I was mixed up with a group of guys who I was trying to impress so as to fit in. They had me doing their dirty work, putting myself in harm's way, laundering money, and being a real trickster. I felt like I should stand up to them or leave the group, but I didn't have the guts. I was letting myself down, had no self-respect, and was doing myself a severe disservice by going along with them. People have been walking all over me in this life, too, and I saw the connection. I needed to stand up for and take care of myself better, because my intentions toward myself have never been right. Since then, things have changed because I broke the cycle. I respect myself a lot more and work only with good people who respect me too.'*

You can identify 'negative' karma occurring in your life when adverse or unpleasant cycles seemingly repeat. These might be relationship problems, career hurdles, or other similar unfavorable circumstances. Karma can seem like bad luck following you around. For example, if you repeatedly find yourself in confrontational circumstances, perhaps you have unhelpful intentions toward yourself, in that you're willing to accept unacceptable behavior from others. If you notice that you keep encountering greedy people, there may be a karmic reason for this in your past. It may be that, at some point, you intentionally shared money unequally with someone who was supposed to receive a fair share. It sounds quite like manifesting, doesn't it? Karma may be another way to perceive the law of attraction in action, where the vibration in which you're stuck creates your reality.

Once we base our choices and actions on beneficial concepts such as love for both the self and others, understanding, forgiveness, sovereignty, and compassion, we no longer accumulate negative karma, and we keep sailing in a positive direction. Sure, one day we might unintentionally upset or hurt someone, but it's the intention that counts, so it doesn't accumulate karma.

If we haven't reconciled our karma during one lifetime, many believe that it spills into the next. Hence, karmic cycles continue to arise until we learn the lessons they bring and amend our intentions and actions. Long cycles of prosperity and satisfaction then set in; this is your positive karma coming back around. Yes, positive karma also exists, very much so, and many people forget this. However, karma is just karma – it's merely that we perceive it positively or negatively.

If there is a karmic cycle apparent in your life that has no discernable cause from your current lifetime, after thoroughly exploring your shadow content through inner work, consider exploring previous lives. You can do so with past-life regression, either with a past-life therapist (for hypnosis), a past-life psychic reading, guided meditation hypnosis, or you can gently explore past lives using your intuitive knowing.

You can heal past-life karma by first identifying the repetitious cycle within the previous lifetime and seeing if there is a similar pattern in your own life. Then, you can examine what karma is trying to teach you. What were your intentions toward yourself and others? What effect did your actions have on all parties involved? Then, after fostering forgiveness for your past-life self and others, and amending your intentions and actions in this lifetime, the cycle begins to release. You can change old routines and patterns of behavior, take a new direction, and base your actions on understanding, forgiveness, compassion, and love.

Ways to Know You're Remembering a Past Life

Many of us have a vague recollection of past lives, yet we tend to disregard it as imagination or irrelevant feelings. Have you ever had a particularly vivid dream of dying? Or perhaps you've dreamed of being a character in ancient times or even some futuristic adventurer traveling the galaxy. In my past-life regression practice, many clients have 'regressed' to future lifetimes. Given the nonlinear nature of time, this may be possible. Perhaps they were experiencing existences so far in advance of our own, that even if they occurred in our past, we would perceive them as the future. Following are some of the ways to know you might be remembering a previous or future lifetime:

◉ You feel drawn to a particular location that seems incredibly familiar, like home, or evokes strong, unexplainable emotion.

◉ When visiting a museum or researching history, you're strangely fascinated with a specific era that seems strikingly familiar.

- You have dreams, especially recurring ones, in which you are someone else, living another life.

- You feel there should be people in your life who are not. You don't consciously remember who they are, yet you know they are missing.

- You have skills and knowledge that you were never exposed to or taught.

- You like to dress in old-fashioned or futuristic clothing.

- You are especially fascinated with sci-fi because it makes better sense than earthly life, and you often daydream of traveling amongst the stars.

- You intuitively feel like Earth is not your original home.

- When you are very relaxed, you have spontaneous memories of places you've never visited or people you've never met. You brush them off as a vivid imagination.

All these instances are subtle rememberings or intuitive feelings arriving from deep within, yet just because they are vague, it doesn't mean they're not real. We can explore them further, get to know ourselves better, and heal anything that requires it.

> 'I had a past-life regression in which I was a rich woman in Asia, about a thousand years ago. I wore the finest clothing, adorned with gold and diamond jewelry, and lived in a large house with many fine possessions. My husband was very powerful, and we had four sons. There was a great war, and my sons went out to lead entire legions.

But none of them returned from battle, and I was utterly heartbroken. The feelings I experienced reminded me of how I feel in my own life. I have always been overprotective of my family, especially of my children, and could never understand where my fears came from. Perhaps now I do.'

You can use the following exercise to explore and heal past lives.

🦋 EXERCISE: PAST-LIFE REGRESSION 🦋 SELF-HYPNOSIS

Our higher self remembers everything. In performing regression, we connect with it to receive memories via the four clairs. Try to complete the whole process in one sitting, but if you need to stop, simply open your eyes, and take a few moments to center yourself back in this reality. Read the process through a couple of times, to remember the story-like structure.

1. Put on some meditation music and sit or lie down comfortably. Close your eyes, listen, and relax into the music for about 15 minutes. Allow thoughts to float away.

2. Set your intention for regression, such as to identify circumstances affecting you today or simply to explore.

3. Visualize or sense a healing, golden light forming around your body. Remain very present in it for about five minutes more, and feel it warming and relaxing each part of your body in turn, paying particular attention to your facial muscles and shoulders. Take as much time as you need.

4. Mentally reach out to your higher self with love.

5. Visualize yourself standing at the top of 10 steps. At the bottom, you'll find a beautiful doorway to one of your past lives.

6. Walk down the steps, counting them down from 10 to one to deepen your meditation further.

7. Once you're at the bottom of the steps, approach the door and observe it. When you're ready, open it, walk through, and close it behind you. Know that it will be right behind you as soon as you wish to leave.

8. Allow your surroundings to form. Stay calm and relaxed and take your time. Avoid choosing, deciding, or guessing, just observe visions forming, or sense or just know what's around you.

9. Take plenty of time to explore and ask yourself some questions. Allow the answers to simply arrive in your mind.

   ~ Am I male or female?

   ~ How old am I?

   ~ Who am I?

   ~ What is the date or approximate time era?

   ~ What do I do in this life?

   ~ Is there anyone else around? If so, who?

   ~ What is going on?

   ~ How do I feel emotionally?

10. When you feel your session drawing to a close, turn around and see the door behind you. Go through, close it, and begin

to climb the 10 steps back to the present. Count each step as you climb.

11. If you found no circumstances that require healing, then draw the session to a close and open your eyes when you're ready. If you did find something, then, simply by becoming aware of it, you have already taken steps toward healing. Well done. Continue to meditate.

12. Simply visualize your past-life self in front of you, standing within a white space.

13. Thank and embrace them and tell them you love them. Send healing love energy from your heart to theirs with the intention of ending the cycle and healing your soul's journey.

14. Allow the scene to fade and open your eyes when you're ready.

Seek the company of others for support if needs be. Such a process can be very cathartic, so take time to integrate your experiences and perform self-care. I hope that in performing this process you can clear some aspects that no longer serve you and go ahead and thrive.

Manifesting the Best Life

Creation matches our thoughts, beliefs, and vibration with circumstances and events that suit them, so if we heal those, we manifest better. Many try to game the system with temporary solutions and end up with only limited or short-term results. We can permanently shift our thoughts, beliefs, and vibration to a more advantageous state without the need for repetitious visualizations, constant affirmations, the use of vision boards, or putting too much effort into it. The basis of manifesting is that it should be effortless, because when we try too hard, we put up walls of resistance against failing. When we pin our hopes and happiness on the outcome too much, we generate fear of failure. Therefore, failure is what we create.

Imagine that reality mirrors your inner world. If you are anxious about upcoming events, Creation is more likely to give you circumstances to cause you anxiety. If you desperately need peace and quiet, your neighbor will put on loud music. When you believe that money is tricky to come by, your hard work won't pay off. When you think you'll never find your soulmate, all your dates will be abysmal. And while you desperately try to get pregnant, parenthood will be elusive. I have seen this many times. When a couple tries for a child for years, it is often when they give up all hope that they get pregnant. I'm not saying that giving up is the solution for every parent-to-be, but it's interesting what happens when we release resistance.

Manifesting Seamlessly

We often manifest from our core beliefs, both helpful and limiting, which we pick up throughout our lifetime. Later, in Chapter 8, I'll provide ways to heal those. But, what if you could maintain a high vibration for manifesting before you've had a chance to perform your inner work? You'd allow Creation the opportunity to bring you positive experiences right now. More happy catalysts, please! I have a valuable shift in thought for you here, one that has the power to improve your manifesting immediately and permanently. It's a switch in perception, a changing of the mind, a transformative point when manifesting becomes a whole lot easier. And here it is:

Let go.

Really? Yes! Yes, you can. We often cling too tightly to every aspect of life, trying to control everything, every little outcome, process, or timing. In minding everything and pinning it all down, we exist in a constant state of resistance to what might happen. 'If I don't complete this on time, we might lose income!' 'Your parents probably won't like me.' 'I think I'm going to get ill.' 'We must get there on time.' 'What if we forget something?' 'What if our plane is delayed?' What if, what if, what if! How about releasing it all?

I'm not implying you should let go of all your desires and aims in life – far from it. But I am suggesting that you release your *dependence* on your goals to provide your happiness and well-being. Of course, they are important, and your consciousness wants forward motion and achievement. Still, it's counterproductive to immerse yourself in the unhelpful emotions that accompany intense wanting, desiring, and not-having. Release those, leaving only your awareness of the present moment and the aims that fill you with joy. You are no longer following your joy when you are in a state of intense wanting. *Trying* to manifest, too, has the reverse effect. In the trying, we are not doing, and it creates a wall of not-yet-being-able. Let go, let go, let go. Releasing everything attracts everything positive.

Does anticipating every outcome and worrying about and controlling everything actually help you? It only makes you feel worse, so why put yourself through it? I used to think that I *should* worry about everything because it would motivate me to make sure everything went right. But then I realized I could do only my absolute best, leave it at that, and practice healthy detachment. You can't do more than your absolute best. In doing so, my vibration was no longer up and down like a wavy line, and I manifested a smoother-running, fulfilling life. In letting go, releasing everything, and trusting in Creation to bring you the absolute best, it will.

Releasing Resistance

It sounds like a leap of faith, and it is. If Creation were a fluffy cloud, you'd be lying right back into it. You can't *really* lie on clouds; it stands to reason, you'd fall straight through, and that's why you don't want to do it. But this cloud is different. If you believe it can support you, it will, and it'll carry you to wonderful places and new heights!

What if you can't let go of, say, fear? Fear about someone's health, your well-being, or something terrible happening. If you become the *observer* of the fear, you're stepping outside of it. You can then accept it, care for, and reassure it. Do you see how you move into a high vibrational flow through acceptance as opposed to resistance? No longer are you lost in the fear; instead, you're its healer.

When I first became a mother, I was somewhat overzealous, trying to make sure my child was super safe, ultra well-cared-for, exceedingly entertained, and fed only the most nutritious foods on the planet. Many new mothers are like this, trying to make sure they don't mess up, often overcompensating for something lacking in their childhood. Anyway, I became sure that dogs in the park were a potential hazard for toddlers. I usually love dogs but had managed to propel myself into a state of hypervigilance. So, what happened next? I manifested dogs, lots of them. Dogs running up to us, dogs licking my child's face, dogs knocking her into puddles, dogs chasing her ball, dogs taking her sandwich, and dogs peeing on the picnic basket. It got to a point where I thought I was barking mad. I couldn't take the anxiety of it anymore, and my consciousness simply snapped. I completely let go, exhausted by reasonless fear. And then? No more dogs, not one. Well, occasionally a happy pooch would trot by and greet us for a pat, but apart from that, we had a howling great time.

So you see, while my thoughts were of dogs, my vibration was fear, and I believed that they were all a threat; Creation brought me dogs to challenge me. Obviously, it was what I needed for my consciousness to evolve. But once I transcended the situation, Creation, or indeed my higher self, said 'Great! Lesson learned.' And it was all over. Is there such a pattern appearing in your life? It may not be karma if your intentions and actions are positive. Instead, your expectations and feelings might be manifesting the situation. Consider letting go.

Mind-Boggling Aspects of Manifesting

There is an interesting crossover between future precognition and manifesting. When you've had a thought about someone whom you haven't seen in months, and then you bump into them while out shopping, did you ever wonder if you manifested meeting them or simply had precognition about it? It seems like an uncanny time loop. By thinking about them, you may have manifested them. But if you were destined to meet them, was it, therefore, precognition? It's like the chicken and the egg. Which came first? Maybe it's both, and what we observe is perhaps Creation creating our reality retroactively, in some way, to manifest our experiences effectively.

The philosophy of retrocausality, or backward causation, is a concept of cause and effect in which an effect precedes its cause in time and so a later event affects an earlier one.'[12] Retrocausality is a pretty cool concept in quantum physics, and implies that what we do today might retroactively alter past events in some way. The possible significance of this is huge when it comes to manifesting. You might wonder how it's possible to change the present or future through thought. Does everything get altered and moved around? How does Creation do it? Consider that our intelligent, energetic reality, can rearrange the past to line up events to facilitate what is happening now, that it rewrites the past, to produce easily what we are manifesting now. We wouldn't remember the old version of events because they no longer existed. Instead, we only remember the new 'timeline' we have jumped on. The whole show continually changes for everybody to most accurately match everyone's thoughts, beliefs, and vibration, and Creation has infinite resources to do so. It's only us humans who believe in lack and limitation.

Thank You, Universe

Gratitude for all that you have and experience in life is also a wonderful manifester. In the vibration of gratitude and appreciation, you manifest even more to be thankful for. We often overlook everyday things – a beautiful picture, a bird's song, even the ability to see or hear these things. Gratitude for our home, no matter what it looks like, our family and close friends, such gratitude manifests even more to appreciate. We can even be thankful for problems (remember we can reframe them as challenges) because they allow us to practice finding solutions, to think outside the box, and to transcend, learn, and grow. Part of manifesting a fulfilling life is not minding having challenges, and the beauty of this is that, in adopting this mind-set, they occur less often!

In trusting the universe, we agree that anything is possible. Do you feel resistance to the thought that anything is possible? If Creation is willing to change the past, present, and future to match your thoughts, beliefs, and vibration, then yes, anything is possible. You can't *make* yourself believe; belief arises, for most people, through evidence. But the more we manifest little improvements and beneficial outcomes, the more proof we receive. So you can start small by performing a quick visualization, and you can adapt this for other scenarios. Next time you need a parking space, just before you arrive, visualize yourself happily driving into a big space. Remember to imagine the feeling of satisfaction, because emotion fuels manifesting. See how often this works. I successfully find an extra-large or double space every time now, which is lucky because I've never been very good at parking. (That's limiting belief right there!)

Taking Action to Create

Manifesting doesn't imply that we achieve a high vibration, heal limiting beliefs, let go, then sit on the sofa doing nothing. The process involves taking action to create. Sometimes action is not needed, like when we unexpectedly manifest a sum of money into our bank account. But often, action is necessary. How will you create a successful business if you don't do any work at all? Because the world appears physical, we tend to forget that it is actually energy. If we want to achieve results, we must work this intelligent energy, change it, and manage it. It's as if we had a magic wand, which is merely an extension of our undistorted, unhindered will. As infinite soul consciousness, you are a co-creator within this energetic reality, not just a passive bystander. You have the power not only to create with your hands, words, and deeds but also via your limitless mental and emotional resources. Marry these together, both physical and mental manifesting, and your potential to create is infinite. We often rely on Creation to manifest everything for us, while forgetting that we *are* Creation. Therefore, we are part of the manifesting process.

> *'I have always been successful in what I do because there's never a question in my mind that I won't be. There are no doubts for me. I set my sights on something and just keep going until I achieve it.'*

In Chapter 9, I'll provide a practice for transcending, which will help you achieve a state of 'letting go.' But if you feel you are already reaching such a state, you can perform the following one-off visualization to send a clear picture to Creation of the version of reality you are manifesting for yourself and others in love and light.

🦋 EXERCISE: MANIFESTING VISUALIZATION TOOL 🦋

Remember always to approach spiritual work with the attitude of playful enjoyment.

1. Meditate for 10 minutes to calm and connect. During this time, imagine yourself on a beautiful beach or in glorious nature; this provides a focal point and helps you to relax. Then allow the visualization to fade.

2. Set the intention to create reality by stating, 'My highest joy is in every moment,' and let go of everything else.

3. Visualize what you are creating. Like a purposeful daydream, imagine yourself fulfilling your aim. Do this in the first person, *being* yourself, not observing yourself. Avoid getting too specific, or you'll limit Creation's ability to create. For example, if you're manifesting a partner, try not to specify hair color or their profession because you never know who will be a better match for you. Creation knows.

4. Feel what it is like to experience this reality. Emotion is the fuel; it's your vibration and sets the tone. *Really* feel it.

5. Close down the visualization after about 30 seconds.

6. Put it to one side in your mind and try not to return it. (When we revisit, we undo.)

7. Carry on, content in the knowledge that the energetic code of reality is realigning itself!

Joy in the Now

❛ *My highest joy is in every moment.* ❜

What a fantastic attitude to take, and without repeating lots of affirmations to yourself, you can choose to take this attitude. It simply reminds you to relax, let go, and trust that your highest joy is manifesting right now.

When we manifest as if our dreams are coming true *soon*, they will always be in the future, constantly out of reach like a donkey following a carrot. Instead, while we're trusting, and releasing resistance, our trust must extend around this present moment; otherwise, our joy will perpetually be in the future.

∼

Chapter 8

Inner Work to Raise Your Vibration

The spiritual path shows us many ways to raise our vibration, and when we do so, joyful and creative days become the norm. We step into our true abilities and become a beacon of inspiration, compassion, light, and energy.

In continuing to guide you humbly through spiritual awakening and beyond, let's go within, into your inner world. For humanity to evolve in a positive direction, ideally, we should all become aware of our inner world. Indeed, for many, it's too painful to look inwardly, because their ego fears what it might find. The ego is happy in its illusions, concealing the true nature of the self. Yet, like an onion, we can peel away certain layers of self, perhaps ones of hurt, suffering, and misfortune, until we reach a core, that place where it all began. The part of the self that *was*, before anything ever happened. And from that core, we start again. Your eyes might water just thinking about it. Yet, what a liberating experience to remove all that which no longer, and perhaps never did, serve a positive purpose – layers between us and happiness, those we no longer wish to keep.

In healing our inner self, the outside world begins to seem friendlier, easier to create and to manage. We experience pleasant emotions more often, instead of being triggered by this and that or waking up in the morning unable to face our responsibilities. I find that sympathetic and attentive inner work is the most long-lasting and effective way to raise your vibration. We heal the deepest levels of our psyche, from which our overall vibration arises.

The Conscious and Subconscious Minds

Before we begin, it's necessary to become acquainted with the functions of both the conscious and subconscious minds because inner healing involves, to a great degree, our conscious mind initiating healing within our subconscious mind.

The conscious mind:

- is your logical processing mind

- holds short-term memory

- interacts with the world

- processes what's going on in the world

- does one thing at a time

- saves information to the subconscious mind

The subconscious mind:

⊚   is your bigger, deeper mind

⊚   stores long-term memories and remembers everything (although poor retrieval of memories can lead us to believe we can't remember)

⊚   stores past programming and beliefs

⊚   is the source of your emotions, imagination, creativity, and intuition

⊚   performs millions of processes at once

⊚   automatically serves the conscious mind with memories, emotions, and responses based on beliefs

Here's an example of conscious to subconscious learning and storing. You consciously learn to ride a bike. It can be tricky, but once you get the hang of it, you naturally store the skill within your subconscious mind for later. When you ride a bike again, you do so easily without really thinking about it. Your subconscious mind just makes it happen. While you're riding, you can even think of other things or enjoy the view. It's the same with swimming, driving, or learning a language. Once you know how, you just do it without thinking about it. All your life experiences are stored within your subconscious mind, whether they were enjoyable and beneficial or the complete opposite. The thing is, much of the content of your subconscious mind unknowingly and unconsciously colors and influences your life today. Until, of course, you become conscious of it.

Healing Limiting Beliefs

Your higher self is beyond the realms of limiting beliefs and knows that anything is possible. You'd be amazed at what you've picked up during your lifetime that affects how you feel about yourself and your reality today, therefore influencing how you live your life. In becoming your true self, brimming with confidence, motivation, and potential, you can heal all within your subconscious mind that requires it.

What Are Core Limiting Beliefs?

Our core beliefs begin to form in childhood. Children are like little sponges, soaking up beliefs and programming from their caregivers, friends, society, events, and circumstances around them. They do this because they are born into a confusing world, filled with uncertainty that they must learn to navigate. Children observe and learn from others and their surroundings as they gain the tools they need to cope and succeed, and diligently build formulas of cause and effect to create a picture of what to expect in the future. All this is stored subconsciously.

Core beliefs are deeply ingrained beliefs, both helpful (liberating) and unhelpful (limiting), that form the core, or basis, of how we perceive and interact with the world. Most of these assumptions we create subconsciously without consciously thinking about them too much. Here are some examples of limiting beliefs we can form in childhood and how they arise:

◉ If I make a suggestion, sometimes others think I'm stupid. Therefore, I should keep quiet.

- My parents argue about money, so money must be scarce and difficult to obtain.

- When I said I wanted to be an artist, they told me to get my head out of the clouds. Therefore, my dream is not worthwhile, and my ambitions are futile.

- I must eat, dress, and generally do as grown-ups tell me, and when I request otherwise, I am naughty. Therefore, decisions are not for me to make.

- I see that my mother has disagreements with many people. Therefore, people are generally difficult and disagreeable.

- My parents are not there for me. Therefore, I must look after myself. No one cares about me.

As you can see, we readily absorb limiting beliefs in our younger years. Positive beliefs, of course, also arise frequently:

- I spent time preparing my presentation, and it went well. Therefore, putting in the effort gets results.

- If I have a problem, my friends and family are always willing to help me. Therefore, people are generally trustworthy and supportive.

We continue to adopt limiting beliefs into adulthood:

- My business projects failed. Therefore, starting a business is extremely challenging.

- My ex-husband continually criticized my capabilities. Although I know he was emotionally manipulative, there must have been some truth in his words.

⊚ Advertising portrays beauty as a priority, often showing successful, good-looking men and women. Therefore, to be acceptable, I must spend time and money to look as good as they do. It is useful to compare myself to others to ensure I measure up.

We also tend to adopt limiting beliefs about reality due to the structure of our societal system, through media, culture, education, and more. They shape our concept of what is possible and can either enhance or limit our ability to create a better way of life. Societal assumptions based on scarcity, competition, disconnection, separation, cold hard logic, and other examples of extreme polarity stop us from innovating in new directions. In retaining such assumptions, we seal ourselves firmly within the earthly illusion, preventing ourselves from imagining beyond it. Limiting beliefs become our reality.

Why Release Limiting Beliefs?

If we rewrite unhelpful beliefs, our confidence, self-image, and self-esteem can increase, allowing us to thrive and fulfill our dreams. Can you see how limiting beliefs are barriers around the mind? These barriers create resistance. Resistance is the 'no' we experience toward something, the unpleasant emotion that arises when we face certain people or circumstances. If I perceive that people with a background like mine usually find it difficult to create abundance, then I won't have the confidence to aim very high. If I believe that others can succeed, then so can I, and I'm more likely to find the means and motivation to make my dreams a reality.

I managed to heal a limiting belief that I didn't even know I had. I struggled with social anxiety from around the age of 14 and thought it was normal to feel that way, and that other people just hid it well. I learned to hide it, too, but underneath my calm, sociable exterior, I was a quivering wreck. I eventually realized that not everyone felt the same way, but I had no idea *why* it was happening to me. I sat with the feeling during a meditation session one day and allowed memories to fill my mind. I was trying to find the root cause because it occurred to me that my subconscious mind might be running a program that resulted in me resisting social interactions to prevent something terrible from happening. I was sitting with the anxiety, but also began to feel hints of fear – of humiliation, ridicule, exclusion – like I was ridiculous and unwanted, perhaps hated. There it was! *I feel like people hate me! Whether I meet them for the first time, or whether they get to know me, they will surely dislike me sooner or later.* Now, why would I feel like people hate me? Consciously I know I'm a nice person, striving to be kind and helpful, so why would anyone feel that way? There's no evidence of this happening today.

Memories began to fill my mind of when that feeling began. One memory was of being on the hockey pitch at school. I'll note now that this story might seem insignificant to some. But, no matter what has happened in your life, if any experience has resulted in significant emotional disturbance, then it can adversely affect your well-being in the future, especially when comparable circumstances arise.

Back to the hockey pitch. Earlier on, I had seen one of the older girls, the most popular one by far, burying a hockey ball in the immaculately maintained ground, right outside the white line. The teacher noticed the buried ball and called everyone over. She proceeded to tell us that no one would go home until someone owned up to the crime or informed her of who had done it. I was only 11 at the time and hadn't yet grasped the concept of not ratting out 13-year-old 'superiors' because you're likely to put yourself in the firing line. Unfortunately, I was rather naive. Being ravenously hungry, I wanted to go home and resented the fact that I'd been standing there for 10 minutes because of a girl who'd never been nice to me anyway. So I put my hand up and pointed out the culprit. At least five older, taller girls, of the domineering type, turned and threw a look of sheer disgust at my very existence. *Oh no*, I thought, *I should have kept my mouth shut.* In addition, oh boy, should I ever have, because from that day forward, they seriously had it in for me. I felt like the walking ridiculed. My own friends were fine, but the rest of the older kids soon found out about it. So I spent the following few years hating school and trying to avoid at least thirty different kids, who all very obviously and openly hated my guts with a vengeance, sometimes aggressively.

I was sure I had located one of the causal experiences for my limiting belief that 'people hate me,' because this memory was one that popped into my mind while I was being present with my current-day emotions. Also, when I recalled it, and other more impactful memories regarding different aspects of my younger life, I began to have an emotional release, which is an energetic catharsis, often a sign that you've struck a nerve and found a cause. Today, having realized and healed this limiting belief (I'll provide techniques shortly), I can foster close friendships without the expectation that people will dislike me sooner or later. I no longer feel the need to protect myself emotionally by running away. In turn, in my higher vibration, I regularly manifest new, meaningful friendships.

Limiting beliefs cause us to manifest a limited version of reality, and liberating positive beliefs help us to manifest the absolute best. It's worth remembering, however, that some limiting beliefs can actually be useful. If you're sure that it's dangerous to swim in the sea during a storm, this isn't limiting you from fulfilling your true potential; it's protecting you from harm. Likewise, if you want to heal a belief such as 'this relationship will never work,' consider that the relationship might actually be a destructive one. What we're addressing here are beliefs that are holding you back in some way and limiting your opportunities.

Good-bye Limits, Hello Possibilities

So, how do you identify and heal limiting beliefs? Half of the healing is already done once you realize the source of your pain, because your subconscious mind, at last, feels like you are listening.

You can make conscious your unconscious beliefs so that you can question them. In shining the light of awareness on traumatic memories, you can see them for what they are, and not how you perceived them in the past. The older, wiser you will likely view such circumstances differently, with greater understanding and, therefore, forgiveness, lessening the burden of guilt and shame on the self. You don't have to carry the programming with you anymore, allowing it to affect how you feel today and how you manifest your reality.

🦋 Exercise: Identifying Limiting Beliefs 🦋

First, we'll identify a limiting belief and then work on healing it. Have a pen and paper ready. You can refer back to this framework as you go.

1. Meditate for 15 minutes, allowing your subconscious mind to come through. Answers will then arise more easily. Relax, let go, and allow.

2. Write down answers to any of the following questions that resonate with you.

   ~ Do you feel held back in some way? If so, how?

   ~ Do you feel unmotivated or blocked from doing something? If so, what are you trying to do?

   ~ What aspects of yourself, if any, do you view poorly?

   ~ Do you experience unpleasant emotions in certain situations? If so, what emotions and in which situations?

3. Take one of your answers and contemplate the limiting belief behind it by adding, 'Because I believe' to it. The answer that comes after this phrase will likely be your limiting belief. For example:

   ~ I want to find a new job but can't get motivated because I believe the right one isn't out there for me (resulting in poor manifesting).

   ~ I want to be single and work on myself for a while, but then again I don't want to because I believe I'll be lonely (a belief that could limit self-development).

~ I get nervous in meetings because I believe I don't have as much to contribute as everyone else.

~ I feel anxious driving since my accident because I believe it will happen again.

~ I struggle in social situations because I believe I don't know how to relate to other people.

If you were to take your limiting belief and use it as an affirmation, you'd be programming your subconscious mind with the exact opposite of what you want to achieve, right? This is, in effect, what a limiting belief does. For all the time we hold on to it, we are reaffirming it, and it continues to reflect in our reality. Instead, we can begin to heal the limiting belief by finding its cause, perceiving it differently, reversing it, and taking some action.

❧ EXERCISE: HEALING LIMITING BELIEFS ❧

1. Remaining relaxed, at the top of a new page write down your chosen limiting belief from the previous exercise, such as, 'No one cares about me,' or 'I will never have much money.' (These beliefs don't exactly help with positive manifesting).

2. Be present in this belief, relax, and ask yourself, 'Where does this belief come from?'

3. Allow an answer to arise from your subconscious mind as a sense of knowing or an inner voice. Your subconscious knows the answers. For example:

~ The belief that no one cares about me comes from my family always being preoccupied with other things.

~ The belief that I will never have much money comes from my father always worrying and complaining about money.

4. Reevaluate the belief. Depending on what it is, choose one or more of the following questions and write down all the answers that come to you.

~ How can I change or improve my circumstances, routines, skills, or practices to help?

~ If I adopted a belief about reality from someone else, how is the belief inapplicable to me? How can I approach life differently than they do?

~ If someone instilled a limiting belief in me about myself, were their words appropriate? How were they misguided? Were they qualified to tell me who I am?

5. Take time to understand events. Were they outside of my control? Are they likely to happen again if I put appropriate measures in place?

6. Consider how events were not my fault.

With this new understanding, your limiting belief can naturally evaporate. You're gaining new perspectives, therefore, rewriting your perceptions.

7. Now, write your limiting belief in the positive. You can use it as an affirmation to reassure your subconscious mind or a motto to live by, for example:

~ 'No one cares about me' is now, 'I am worthy of love and care.'

- ~ 'I will never have much money,' is now, 'I have an abundant life.'

- ~ 'I don't know how to relate to people' is now, 'I am learning how to relate to people.'

- ~ 'I believe I'll be lonely,' is now, 'I am strong and independent.'

Healing limiting beliefs is a form of inner work, so let's go in to it a little deeper.

Inner Work

Our inner world is vast and dynamic. It's an amalgamation of perceptions, beliefs, assumptions, programming, and memories both pleasant and unpleasant. But it's precisely those unpleasant memories – the ones we'd rather forget – that tend to affect us still. Sometimes we struggle to pinpoint the sources of our pain, and many people don't even realize it's beneficial to do so.

I use the term *subconscious programming* to describe assumptions we make about reality that arise through experience and cause us to perform behaviors to avoid similar new experiences or to offset emotional pain arising from them. Sometimes programming coincides with limiting beliefs. If a child receives a telling off every time they make a mistake, a limiting belief might arise that 'I am bad when I make a mistake.' Children make plenty of mistakes while they are trying to master tasks; it's part of the learning process. But, in response, such a limiting belief might also create programming for certain behaviors to avoid the same unpleasant experiences in future. The child wants to avoid the telling-off, so instead of risking making another mistake, they'll avoid trying new tasks altogether.

> *'Every time my partner raises his voice, even a little, I flinch and want to run away. Of course, disagreements happen, but to me, it seems like he's angry when he's not. I know where my sensitivity and urge to flee come from. It reminds me of how I used to feel when my parents would scream and shout at each other.'*

An unhelpful program such as this can result in us having to avoid any intense discussion altogether or even being completely unable to defend ourselves. We can address this kind of automatic response with inner work.

Emotional Signposts

Our past experiences also give rise to *emotions* that we experience in the present day. Your history produces your perception of today's experiences. Every positive emotion we have is us being fully able to enjoy the moment without any resistance to what's going on. But every unpleasant emotion is a signpost from the subconscious that we are not coping well with the situation. The signpost is a helpful indication of an opportunity for healing.

The next time you feel sadness, despair, anxiety, guilt, fear, resentment, annoyance, or anything similar, instead of pushing your feelings away because you want to feel good again, welcome these feelings and listen. Time after time, people find that in doing this, unpleasant feelings fade away more quickly and return less often. So in accepting (not resisting) our emotions, we're listening to what they're trying to say, and this is the first step in healing them (further steps will be discussed shortly).

Your subconscious mind wants you to listen, and if you're not, it'll only shout the emotions louder. Unhealed traumas start to turn up in our dreams, in flashbacks, and even breakdowns. Your inner world hopes more than anything that you'll acknowledge, validate, and accept all it's trying to tell you. It's communicating with you. For example, if you feel anxious before a networking event, your palms are sweaty, and you feel dizzy, then your subconscious mind is likely resisting what's coming up. It's trying to protect you from painful humiliation and embarrassment because you've felt these feelings before in similar circumstances, perhaps when you were younger or less equipped to handle the situation. Your inner world says, 'No don't do it. You'll experience pain!'

Your subconscious mind is trying to protect you. Fear is to protect you from danger and anxiety from lots of things, like the unknown. Your guilt is trying to protect you from performing more actions you perceive as your fault, and from shame of being a 'bad person.' The terrible trouble is that, although you have this super protector within you, it often has the wrong idea. If you experience shame, you feel you are 'bad' in some way. But what if you're not? Often, those who do experience shame are not 'bad' people at all. What if someone trained you to think you were a 'bad person'? Many grew up in conditions where caregivers were exceptionally intolerant and never said anything encouraging. This isn't the fault of the youngster, yet they accepted this terrible limiting belief because kids are very impressionable. Then they carry this shame into their adult life, always perceiving themselves negatively. The subconscious mind accepted a false limiting belief because it didn't know any better.

An unpleasant emotion coming from the past isn't always the result of someone *telling* us who or what we are; it can also result from someone's *inaction*. Those who grew up in neglectful circumstances often end up with poor self-esteem because they feel they are not worth anyone's time. They never received love, validation, acceptance, and inclusion, so they believe they are unworthy of it. It's incredible how often we think that our background was perfectly normal, then, when we grow up and compare it to someone else's, we see that we were missing out or subject to something irregular.

If you had an aggressive parent, you might carry an expectation in to adulthood that other people will be aggressive toward you. The behavior was normalized. Then, because of this expectation, you accept or even undeservedly manifest a partner who is also aggressive, and the cycle continues until you become aware. Often, the cycle is broken when we realize our true self-worth and no longer accept such behavior. But this takes strength. Some sufferers of another's aggression become aggressive themselves as they subconsciously attempt to normalize the behavior.

Finding Resolution

Sadness and depression – undercurrents which many endure every day – also usually have roots in our past. In my experience from working with others, depression often arises due to unresolved loss, grief, or other experiences of which the subconscious mind cannot make sense. We might endure pain over someone's behavior, such a deep disappointment or betrayal that it still haunts us today. We may feel the loss of someone that we have not grieved for properly. We may also grieve for loved ones we have lost contact with, the home we grew up in, a previous job, a group of friends, or a beloved pet. Such loss remains remembered yet unreconciled deep within our mind as it cries out for us to address it consciously and provide closure.

> *There is no light without shadow and no psychic wholeness without imperfection.*
>
> CARL JUNG

We can work toward identifying shadows and healing them, but don't be hard on yourself if it seems to take a long time. We should perform inner work in manageable stages. I've never met anyone who has resolved all their shadow content. Sometimes we need to remember that no one is perfect, neither ourselves nor others, and we can only do our best.

It's always tempting to blame our parents for our suffering. And yes, some parents are indeed the cause of their children's suffering. Yet frequently, it's like the helpless being led by the clueless. Many adults are, in effect, grown-up kids themselves, carrying all their baggage from the past. Most parents don't get to read a manual of how to parent a child effectively, and even if they do, many are so traumatized themselves that it doesn't make much difference. In blaming and resenting our parents, no matter what they did or neglected to do, we only create more negative energy within ourselves. It's in the understanding and forgiveness that we truly heal.

> *'Mom used to drink, and life was pretty tough. Even though I hated her for it for a long time, now I get that she was in pain and completely incapable of being a good mom.'*

Other people's destructive, unkind, or abusive behavior is never acceptable; it should not be tolerated, and we should quickly remove ourselves from such situations (sadly, this is often difficult for a child). However, through understanding others' backstories, we can find at least some forgiveness, which releases a lot of pent-up dark energies. People always behave the way they do for a reason, and that reason is usually found in their unhealed, traumatic past. Their sarcasm, anger, aggression, narcissism, manipulation, and more, arise from their own personal pain. Importantly, we realize that the events of the past were often not our fault and we are not 'bad', and this lifts a tremendous burden from the self. Do you see how, after such a perceptual change, you are more able to draw a line through past events and move forward in a higher vibration? It's like finding freedom, and we are liberated from the past. We perceive ourselves differently and see others and the world with new hope.

The 'You of Today' Takes the Wheel

In a way you are in two minds, the conscious you of today that has evolved and grown into a more mature, able, and empowered person, and your subconscious inner world, which still hangs on to old experiences, trying to protect you from new ones. But in helping your inner self understand that the 'you of today' is taking the wheel, you can better manage your vibration. Your subconscious needs to know that you are more than capable of consciously navigating life and that you don't require warning emotions to ward you away and protect you from life events. In healing your subconscious mind, you can take charge of your emotions. This inner part of you, in turn, begins to trust the 'you of today' and moves into the background so that you can enjoy your life to the full, reveling in positive emotions.

We can break the cycle of suffering – our own personal cycle and the one handed down to us. Our children receive the benefits of our own inner work too. Sometimes we rebel against inner work because it can be painful to face. So we say to ourselves, 'I'm fine,' and soldier on, perhaps medicating or self-medicating. Some things can take a lot to get over, so take it step-by-step with patience and compassion. Through honest and thorough inner work, we can begin to feel more whole and complete by default, even during the difficult times. We can better cope with anything that arises. You can use inner work in conjunction with meditation, affirmations, and other ways to raise your vibration. But inner work is the groundwork, the foundation for permanent healing. Soul retrieval is awesome inner work, and it's coming up soon, because it deserves its own section. But first, here's another helpful inner work technique.

Exercise: Conversations with the Self

You might perceive talking to yourself as strange. But why shouldn't we open a healthy dialogue with ourselves? You'd chat and listen to a friend if they required support, wouldn't you? Who better to understand, trust, and forgive yourself than you? I often experience great comfort and release by doing this, because I know that the answers are within me, and the same is true for you. You have direct access to your inner world, and so long as you're open to exploring new points of view, you can likely provide yourself with sound guidance and advice, just like you would a friend.

Have a pen and paper ready. Getting your thoughts out on paper has the added benefit of allowing the paper to hold any worries or anxieties, so you don't have to. The aim of this practice is to make friends with your subconscious mind while remembering it's part of you. Stop the process if you experience any overwhelming emotions and seek some support. Write everything down as you go.

1. Relax or meditate for about 15 minutes to allow your subconscious mind to come through. Then open your eyes and work through the next steps.

2. Just allow your most prominent emotional challenge to arise. Feel it for a few moments.

3. Mentally separate into two people;

    ~   the conscious you of today, the person you have grown into and become

~ the inner subconscious part of you, your inner world, including your inner child, hurt younger self, or any other personas that have arisen over time

4. Be the conscious you of today. Start by asking your subconscious mind, 'How can I help?' and wait for a response. You might experience an emotion, memories, your inner voice, or a sense of just knowing what you need to heal. Write down what you receive.

5. Imagine you are a counselor encouraging someone to open up more about how they feel. From the following list, choose the most appropriate questions or ask ones of your own. Await the responses.

~ How do you feel? When was the first time you began feeling this way?

~ What is the challenge you are experiencing? When did it begin?

~ How did this event unfold (if at all)? How likely are such events to happen again?

~ Has anyone else played a role? If so, how? What understanding of this person's background do you have that may have resulted in their behaviors? (You're not excusing their behaviors, instead you're making sense of them).

6. Move on to encouraging your inner self to find answers and allow them to arise intuitively. You can ask:

~ Imagine the best solution, what would it be?

~ What kind of positive, constructive action would be beneficial?

~ What would it take for you to find happiness?

7. Now you can advise your inner self, and this is up to you. The following framework may help, remembering that understanding leads to forgiveness:

~ Provide a greater understanding of how and why events unfolded as they did, or why other people may have acted as they did, lessening the burden of shame or guilt on yourself.

~ Provide reasons for releasing past events and finding forgiveness for yourself and others as far as you can.

~ Encourage your inner self to release the past, draw a line through it, and move forward in love, power, and peace.

~ Reassure your inner self that you, the conscious you of today, is taking the wheel and is capable of managing life effectively.

8. Thank your subconscious mind.

Soul Retrieval

Soul retrieval is an ancient shamanic practice. I offer you a particular technique, adapted so that you can perform it yourself, that I use during hypnosis sessions. Shamanic practitioners have found that pieces of the self are left behind during emotionally charged or traumatic past events. It's as if our energy splinters off and remains in such times and places due to the emotional shock of the particular events or circumstances. These pieces are called soul fragments, and we can reintegrate them. They are unlikely to be actual fragments of our soul, although it can feel that way because, if we leave too much of our energy behind, we can feel drained or even incomplete. We may also leave energy fragments behind in previous lifetimes.

> 'In my early twenties, I didn't want to be part of my family's religion anymore. My parents were furious and threw me out of the house. The rejection was terrible, and I felt completely worthless for years. Lately, I discovered a method to go back to that time and view the events in a new light. Not only that, but I also took back a part of myself that filled, what felt like, a hole in my heart.'

Part of our spiritual journey is working toward becoming more emotionally whole and complete so that other people have less emotional influence over us. They no longer dictate how we feel, and this goes for unfortunate events, too, even if no people were involved.

Soul retrieval works in two ways. Not only are we metaphysically retrieving our energy, but we are also sending an important message to our subconscious mind – that of closure. Whenever we perform hypnosis (the art of being very relaxed and accessing our subconscious mind), we aim to perceive events in new ways to unburden the self; this is not blame-shifting but fostering forgiveness for the self, others, and situations. We aim to heal the past so that our conscious self of today can take the wheel and move forward in power and potential. We grow closer to becoming our true self.

> 'When I was nine, I was playing in the field while my little brother was climbing the old oak tree. Mom had told me to watch him, and I did ask him to be careful. I didn't think he would actually fall, but he did and broke his leg. He was screaming in unbelievable pain, and I remember being so shocked that I just stood there staring, not knowing what to do. My mother was crazily angry that I allowed him to climb so high, and I've carried incredible guilt about it, especially as he still has nerve damage to this day. Soul retrieval allowed me to see the event in a new way. I saw that I wasn't old enough to take proper care of another child, and that I shouldn't have received all the blame. I collected the energies that I lost due to the shock and guilt, and feel ready to move on without feeling like I was the cause of his pain.'

We might suspect we have left soul energy fragments behind if we:

- frequently experience unpleasant emotions

- are unable to release or 'get over' past events

- feel there is unfinished business

- still have a strong attachment to a place or person

- continually miss someone, something, or a place

- feel incomplete

- feel 'spaced out' after a recent significant event (due to energy loss)

- have unexplained physical pain (due to energy loss or imbalance)

🦋 EXERCISE: THE SOUL RETRIEVAL PROCESS 🦋

We take the emotion we wish to heal and follow it back in time to find the cause of the fragmentation as well as the fragment itself (if there is one, of course). If you already know the cause, you'll still use the emotion to get to the memory.

Read through the process and commit it to memory. Make sure you'll be undisturbed, dim the lights, and lie in a comfortable position. Put on some gentle, soothing meditation music to help align your vibration. If visualization is tricky for you, sense or just know what's going on. Only perform this process if you feel strong enough to do so, and remember, you can stop at any time by opening your eyes. If you wish, use the protective light practice (*see p.179*) for extra strength beforehand.

1. Choose an emotion you'd like to heal and set the intention to find an energy fragment for reintegration.

2. Close your eyes and focus on the music for about 15 minutes. Listen to the individual notes, their tone and vibration. Allow any mental images, feelings, and thoughts that arise to come and go without becoming swept up in them.

3.   Focus on your body for about five minutes, working from head to toe. Allow every muscle to relax fully. Take your time.

4.   Be present in the emotion you'd like to heal. Allow it to grow.

5.   Slowly count down from 10 to one. As you do so, remain entirely present in the emotion and feel yourself going back in time. When you get to number one, say within your mind or out loud, 'Be there now.'

6.   Allow your surroundings to form and observe where you find yourself. Notice colors, objects, people (if any), and what is going on. Take your time.

7.   Allow events to play out for a few moments.

8.   Freeze-frame the memory so that everything is still. If the memory is a painful one, do this immediately before the scene plays out.

9.   Tell any people in the memory how their actions made you feel and the effect it's had on you today. If it's an event without people, speak to it in the same way.

10. Look around for any energy you may have left behind in this past scene. It may appear as a cloud or ball of energy.

11. Send love from your heart toward this energy until it completely transmutes into love.

12. See the energy coming toward you and reintegrating with yourself. Observe how you feel, perhaps a sense of relief, joy, or completeness.

13. Attempt forgiveness. Say 'I forgive you,' and send love and healing energy to the entire scene.

14. Allow the memory to fade. Remaining calm and relaxed, count from one to 10 and open your eyes when you're ready.

Sometimes people cry a little during soul retrieval, and this is a cathartic release. Catharsis can gently continue for a day or two in the form of either feeling sad and down or joyful and liberated. But it's vital to perform self-care, take it easy, allow your emotions to run their course, and seek the support of others if you need to. But afterward, a state of blissfulness can arise, the satisfaction of a job well done, or a feeling of completion. During awakening and beyond, we do experience highs and lows. We face our shadows, heal them, and our vibration rises higher. Gradually, there are fewer shadows as our infinite light illuminates them. As we gain new perspectives through the art of living fully, our perceptions of our past experiences continue to change in further restorative ways.

Chapter 9

Moving Forward

Ever onward and upward, let's explore more concepts for unlocking your innate remembering and broadening your view of the possible. I found that during awakening my mind was like a stew of intriguing information. The stew wasn't quite ready yet, there were still ingredients missing, and it needed to cook longer. But the more morsels of quality knowledge I put into it, the more promise it held, and eventually, out came a unique creation of my own. The more inner- and outer-worldly perspectives you can gather, the more you come up with ideas of your own to incorporate into your life and share with others.

For me, intuitive understanding began to advance upward, like a tree, through the levels of my mind, the roots deep within my soul's remembering, the trunk traversing my subconscious, and the branches growing and multiplying throughout my awareness. My emotions, too, instead of being things that just happened to me, became profound and revealing signs to show

how I was doing at that moment and what I could work on further. My emotional intelligence increased, and my empathy for others deepened. Learning to perceive the world in new ways allowed me to witness the miracle of life and observe the synchronous signs that guide us all toward spiritual evolution.

Before moving forward, let's look at a few situations in which we can become lost, a bit flustered, or a little stuck during spiritual awakening.

Pitfalls to Avoid

Most people have encountered, or at least become a little embroiled in, one or two misconceptions or confusions that impede their energetic flow. Now, it's not my intention to be gloomy, nor am I saying that spiritual life is full of pitfalls and potholes. These issues may never affect you, but it helps to be aware of them so that you can offer some guidance when you encounter them in other people.

We can unwittingly find ourselves performing spiritual bypassing – when we use spiritual concepts to avoid certain situations or aspects of ourselves. It can manifest in various ways:

- In witnessing the suffering of others, we assume they manifested it for themselves or that they chose such circumstances before birth. Therefore, we bypass offering them our compassion and assistance.

- We assume that, in using the law of attraction, we can bypass the need to take action to create.

⊚ We blame physical or emotional health conditions *solely* on electromagnetic or astrological energies, thus bypass seeking healing.

⊚ We rely excessively on our spirit guides and loved ones on the other side of life for direction rather than explore our options and make our own decisions.

⊚ We bypass our boundaries to appear kind, tolerant, or accepting, even in the face of unacceptable behavior.

⊚ We repress unpleasant emotions to force a high vibration, bypassing facing our shadows.

Quick, Look Happy

Some perform spiritual bypassing by trying to force a positive outlook, and because they believe that, as they're on the spiritual path, they're supposed to be in a high vibration right away. They wish to appear happy and balanced; otherwise, others might think they're 'not doing spirituality correctly.' But people are more likely to relate to our authenticity than a carefully maintained veneer of perfection. *Telling* ourselves to be happy doesn't tend to produce happiness. It's precisely in the accepting, sitting with, and listening to our emotions, and performing ongoing inner work, that such feelings subside and lessen. It doesn't matter what people think, and if high vibes elude you today, it's okay; you're still doing your best. Having accepted this, you know that the next moment is a fresh start.

'Life Was Easier Before,' Says the Ego

In terms of general pitfalls, occasionally our ego begins to feel deprived, resulting in feelings of emptiness or frustration. Because your quest for authenticity and soulful dimensions doesn't include pandering to the desires, dramas, and delusions of the ego, its attention starts to stray back toward three-dimensional concerns. It might have found life delightfully distracting as it was, full of short-term pleasures, dopamine rushes, and respite provided by colorfully hypnotizing screens. 'Come back over here,' the ego says, 'it's much simpler and cozier to go back to sleep.' The ego forgets that fulfillment and purpose aren't in the societal paradigm, but such a life suited it best because it had a greater role to play. So if it beckons you back, remember how far you've come and that the ego part of you, although a mere shadow of the shadow it used to be, will still occasionally moan and complain that it has less with which to identify. Thank it for its input, but remind it that you're in the driver's seat now. Yes, you'll still enjoy the earthly world because you do, after all, live here, but it's on your terms now, consciously being and becoming more than physicality has to offer.

My Way or the Highway

Sometimes we come across those who develop quite strong and rigid views about the nature of reality and the most useful approaches to spiritual development. They are creating new frameworks of belief that they perceive as the truth, so, naturally, they think others should adopt them too. I have found that the more I learn, the more I realize what I don't know, so I continually question my previous assumptions just in case they require improvement. It's like walking into a dark unexplored cave, wearing a headlamp that illuminates only a few feet in front of you. The more time you spend exploring the cave, the more you realize just how vast it is. It's the same with knowledge. There's a vast expanse of it out there, and the more you explore, the more you realize there is to explore. So in constructing a firm set of beliefs or rigidly sticking within a current assemblage of knowledge, we only limit ourselves to what is already known, excluding all other possible revelations.

Not My Planet or My Galaxy

Some feel like Earth is not their home and get very down about it. The whole fabric of the place seems alien or at odds with their vibration. They confirm a lifelong suspicion that something is just 'not right' through learning about reincarnation and previous lifetimes. They find that, if they have lived lives 'elsewhere,' then those planets or dimensions are in fact their 'normal'; hence, Earth feels strange.

You may feel like an extraterrestrial on Earth when you struggle to find others on your wavelength. You might have a strong feeling that life on Earth is not how it's supposed to be, as if you've been somewhere better. Or you may be intolerant or allergic to many substances or foodstuffs because they are foreign to your vibration. A longing arises to return to a planet, galaxy, or plane of existence that you vaguely remember or intuitively know is home. Yet there's no point in wishing your life away; you incarnated here for a reason. (We'll look at the potential reason shortly, when we examine purpose.)

If Reality Is an Illusion, What's the Point of Life?

In realizing that all matter, on the most fundamental level, is alive, intelligent energy, many begin to wonder if they are living in an illusion of some kind. More startling still, they may wonder whether reality is merely a dream, and they're making it all up. These kinds of thoughts bring about feelings of emptiness and futility as if their lives have been one big lie. Although our consciousness exists within a seemingly unending sea of energy and information interpreted to produce the reality we see around us, it doesn't make our experience of life any less valid. Whether the world is actually as solid as it seems, or whether it merely appears that way, we are still having a profound experience of life. You are a co-creator within this dimension, co-creating with other beings who share this reality too. We see the evidence in the creations that we and others create – all very valid, all really happening.

I'm Going to Meditate – Actually, I'll Do It Tomorrow

I have spoken to literally hundreds of spiritual seekers who struggle to sit and meditate, and resent themselves for not being able to stick with it. Challenges they encounter include being swamped by unpleasant thoughts, memories, and emotions, feeling fidgety and being unable to settle, or avoiding the process altogether, even though they have a firm intention to do it. If this is you, know that you are not alone and that help is at hand.

Do you think your ego wants to meditate? Seeing as the ego wants more – more distractions, more stuff, more intrigue, more identification – do you think it wants to sit still and disappear? That's what happens to the ego during meditation, and that's the last thing it wants to do. The human ego is not us, it's merely a part, yet it tends to complain the loudest. Your true soulful self loves to meditate, but all too often, the ego gets the last word.

Meditation and mindfulness not only allow us to find the calm, thoughtless space within ourselves but also facilitate our connection with all that is. They're one of the most deep-felt and useful things we can do. Many studies have explored the potential benefits of meditation. It has been found that the human propensity for 'mind-wandering' correlates with the activation of parts of the brain associated with self-referential processing, persistently going over ideas referring to the self. This process is also associated with unhappiness. One study found that the highly active parts of the brain (the default-mode network) responsible for such unhappiness actually calm during meditation. A December 2011 article in *Proceedings of the National Academy of Sciences*, states: *'We found that the main nodes of the default-mode network... were relatively deactivated in experienced meditators across all meditation types.... Our findings demonstrate differences in the default-mode network that are consistent with decreased mind-wandering.'*[13]

So the mind's propensity to go over and over things calms during meditation. This is a proven fact. Knowing this, and researching further advantages of meditation, we can generate motivation to meditate. Now, your ego needs to become accustomed to your new meditation routine. If it gets used to performing meditation and knows when it's happening, then it is more likely to comply. In establishing a consistent meditation routine, your ego knows what you expect. Even if it is for 20 minutes, twice a week, it's a thousand times better than no meditation at all, and your ego realizes it's not going to die, and gives in. Here's a little secret: Your ego will naturally reduce in strength and size through meditation, but as this progress happens slowly, it doesn't tend to notice. You can say, 'Thank you, ego, for your input, but I'm meditating now.'

The best solution for being unable to meditate is to meditate. I know that sounds silly, but if you can get a modest little practice going, your consciousness will begin to love it and actually want more. Before long, you'll be rearranging your schedule to fit in a half-hour daily meditation. But don't expect that of yourself already, because such expectations create frustrations (resistance) associated with failure. Allow your routine to develop naturally on its own. Here are some helpful tips.

- Aim for 20 minutes, twice a week.

- Pick two evenly spaced days, say Sunday and Thursday.

- Choose a time of day for consistency, perhaps always at 8:00 a.m. or 8:00 p.m.

- Sit comfortably with your back straight to prevent slouching, which can make you sleepy. I found that a kneeling meditation stool automatically produces perfect posture.

- Set an intention before you begin. For example, to become a point of pure awareness, or to observe without judgment.

- Have no expectations of your level of achievement, simply follow the joy of doing something beneficial to your well-being.

- To prevent falling asleep, meditate when you feel most awake and alert.

- For mindfulness meditation, become aware of your body, your surroundings, feelings, sounds, and thoughts. Observe without evaluating, as if you were watching them from your point of awareness.

- For concentrative meditation, approach it like a tiger ready to pounce, but balance this with calmness. In this way, you are focused and attentive but not in an active state.

- If thoughts or feelings arise, maintain your point of pure awareness, and see them lovingly go.

- Focus on a 'placeholder' of your choice, for example:

  ~ a moving mental image, such as a tree swaying in the breeze or ocean waves

  ~ an inanimate image such as a light or a symbol

  ~ your breath

  ~ a mantra or affirmation

  ~ counting to 10 and back down again repeatedly

Super Useful Concepts

What better than a collection of mind-expanding concepts to positively augment your perceptions of self, the world, and the metaphysical universe? Such ideas have helped many to make sense of life and dissolve illusions.

As Above So Below

'As above so below,' or as some people say, 'As within so without.' This is the hermetic principle of correspondence. But what does it mean? It implies that the characteristics or laws of our reality apply to both the very large and very small. For example, a helix nebula looks very much like a human eye; the swirling motion of the Milky Way resembles a hurricane; and we find examples of the Fibonacci sequence throughout the natural world on many scales, in the growth patterns of ferns or sunflower seed spirals. We become aware of the same patterns appearing throughout our reality, helping us to understand the nature of things. Rumi is supposed to have said, 'You are not a drop in the ocean, you are the entire ocean in a drop.' Although this may have been a mistranslation, be that as it may, it is still profoundly relevant. It helps to illustrate most clearly our standpoint within the all. Although we may perceive ourselves as 'little me' within an ocean of other beings, ultimately, they and everything else are part of us, within us, because we are all one. We are each the universe reflected in an individual. What an empowering thought. 'As within so without' implies that our outer world mirrors our inner world. So to improve your outer world, you can change your inner world.

A Polarizing Thought

Duality and polarity also help us to perceive life more clearly. *Duality* means to consist of two parts, and *polarity* is the state of having two opposites. (People often use these terms interchangeably regarding spirituality.)

Examples of some poles are:

- hot and cold (temperature)

- safe and dangerous (risk)

- healthy and sick (health)

- Love and hate (feeling about someone or something)

- pride and shame (self-perception)

- Joy and sadness (emotions of well-being)

Imagine a pendulum swinging between one of these sets of poles, and you'll observe that there are many degrees between them. There are many increments between freezing and boiling, or between unconditional love and intense hatred, and often, there is a neutral point in the middle. So these poles are not absolutes; they are varying. They are also the same thing, differing in degree only. The thing is, we are conditioned, especially in the Western world, to think in absolutes instead of seeing things nonjudgmentally for what they are. Of course, we need to test the temperature of our water, evaluate a project, or the strength of our feelings, but when it comes to everyday life, we can transcend much by unifying the poles.

When we automatically reach for judgment, we close the book on a matter and often experience unpleasant emotions along with it. For example, I might judge my house to be shabby and in need of redecoration. I'd like it to be beautiful, but it's not. But, I can unify the poles of this judgment, accept that it is how it is, then work toward improving it if I wish. If there's someone at work whom everyone perceives as disagreeable, thus causing friction, I might instead choose to observe this person without personal judgment. Perhaps I'll see them as someone who has a backstory that I know nothing about, afford them compassion, and then find ways to cooperate with them more effectively or consider other solutions. Therefore, my emotions calm. Notice how many poles you apply in everyday life. If you experience unpleasant emotions, consider seeing things for what they are, such as a home or a person, and then work toward improving matters. You'll reduce distress and unnecessary suffering.

It's worth noting that if duality had an opposite, it would be oneness.

Masculine and Feminine Energies

An understanding of the masculine and feminine helps us to understand ourselves better, enabling our genuine personality to shine through. We're not addressing biological sex, gender, sexual orientation, or saying that 'men are this or women are that.' Instead, we're exploring the universal energies Creation uses to create, and these we call the masculine and the feminine. Each is present within all of us to varying degrees and has the following characteristics:

- masculine energies – drive, will, determination, logic, discipline, stability, structure, power, strength, courage, focus, and boundaries

- feminine energies – emotion, feeling, intuition, creativity, nurturing, sensitivity, reflection, flow, compassion, empathy, patience, and grounding

We can explore our personal balance of each of these energies, and, seeing as they originate from the seat of our soul, we can further discover the nature of our true personality. Some traits, however, may be exacerbated or distorted due to earthly experiences, and we can question the origins of these and attempt to balance them through inner work if we wish.

Allow me to give you an example. Imagine hypothetical male and female partners. The male, in this instance, although masculine in his appearance, pastimes, and interests, has an abundance of feminine energies. He may be rather a dreamer, using his imagination to formulate new creative projects, but often lacks the focus and drive to make them a reality. He might also be highly compassionate, especially aware of other people's emotions, and see poetic beauty in even the ordinary. On the other hand, his partner, although female, tends to exude plenty of masculine energies. Feminine in mannerisms and demeanor, she is the logical one and highly determined to achieve her goals. She plans and sticks to a schedule and, while loving and caring, is less emotionally moved when her partner otherwise would be.

Everyone is different and has a complex balance of masculine and feminine energies. Whatever someone's sex or gender, each is a unique mix.

I have heard men say:

> *'My profession requires quite a logical, left-brained approach, and that always suited me. Facts and information, for me, are the basis for truth. Yet, I found that in nurturing my creativity and emotional side, a*

> *new dimension opened up. I found new aspects of my personality from which I can express more fully who I am and what I mean with sincerity and feeling, further enhancing all that I do.'*

Whether your energies are more toward the masculine or the feminine polarity, you can consider allowing your opposite to shine through here and there. That's if you want to – you might be very content as you are. It's in the awareness of such energies that we can begin to *allow* undiscovered aspects of ourselves to emerge.

Ponder This for a Moment

How often do you sit down to explore your theories on things? Contemplation is not about becoming lost in the involuntary thoughts and emotions that we experience due to an untamed mind; it involves the intentional pondering of concepts we choose to explore. Contemplation is great.

I like to sit and take time to stare at a tree, the sky, or even at my bathroom tiles. I pick a concept and ask lots of questions about it, for instance, how can I get my kids to appreciate each other more? What is beyond this universe? Is there a timeline where I'm doing something else? Why do I feel a little tense today? In mindfully considering such topics, we get to know our own mind and become less reactive to the external world because we've already reviewed some solutions. We also compile a bank of useful opinions to share with others in the midst of conversation, and we're stimulating the knowing, understanding, and embodying process that I explained earlier.

Let's Drink Love

One of the most effective practices I use for physical and emotional well-being is speaking to water, because of its ability to store positive energies. The media raise this topic very seldom, having unsubstantially debunked it to preserve the mainstream narrative. Plenty of research has been performed, however, proving its effectiveness. Why shouldn't we know about the hidden potential of water? Probably because we'd realize our psychic potential and the extent to which our thoughts and emotions energetically affect our world. That's the last thing supporters of our materialistic way of life would like.

Masaru Emoto took samples of distilled water and subjected them to both positive and negative emotions. He and his team then froze the samples and observed the resulting ice crystal formations. They found that samples exposed to pleasant emotions such as love, joy, and compassion showed beautiful symmetrical ice crystals of various configurations. But the crystalline structures of the ice exposed to negative emotions were disorganized, disarranged, and showed little symmetry. The molecules of the water had rearranged themselves to copy the vibrations of the emotions. So it seems that water has a memory, psychically influenced by our thoughts and feelings.

In the documentary *Water, The Great Mystery*, physicist Rustum Roy notes, *'[Water] may be the single most malleable computer.... It's like a computer memory.... The molecular structure is the alphabet of water, and you must make a sentence out of water, and you can change the sentence.'*[14]

You can change the molecular structure of the water by speaking and emoting your intentions toward it, and this energizes it with your positive emotions, as physicist Konstantin G. Korotkov notes in the same documentary: *'It became clear that positive and negative human emotions are the strongest element of influence.... So love increases water's energy levels and stabilizes the water, while aggressive emotions reduce the energy and make radical changes in the water.'*[15]

In consuming fully energized, positively charged water, you're filling your body with high vibrational energy, providing a boost to your well-being. Consider that your body is up to 60 per cent water, the heart and brain 73 per cent, and the lungs 83 per cent. Imagine then, the difference you can make to your health, wellness, and vitality by nurturing self-love. We can work on reducing our negative self-talk, self-resentment, unworthiness, and feelings of not doing or being enough, and instead rearrange the molecules within our cells into beautiful, high vibrational patterns.

The Art of Moving Beyond

Another concept – one which has allowed me to flow with life and overcome challenges – is the art of transcending. It means to move beyond something, often difficulties or limitations. We can apply it to how we feel about certain events, then methodically find solutions to them. Transcending is not denial or disconnection, rather a means for releasing resistance as well as bringing balance to our emotional reaction. If we are having a disagreement with someone who is becoming increasingly angry, we can transcend or move beyond their emotional display so that we do not automatically react with our own heated emotions. You can even visualize moving past it in your mind. After all, it serves no purpose to fuel the fire of someone who is already losing control. Feeding negativity with more low vibrations only exacerbates the situation. Instead, you can take calm action to remedy the situation, to assist the other person, or to maintain your boundaries. It also helps to have understanding of any circumstances, both present and historical, that led this person to become so stressed.

Imagine you have locked yourself out of your house. Your car keys are inside, and you're going to miss an important morning meeting. As you feel your frustrations rising, take a moment to accept your feelings and that the situation has indeed happened. The only thing to do now is to carry on. So take a deep breath and move beyond it, ready to proceed with practical, constructive action.

🦋 Exercise: Transcending 🦋

Sometimes we feel that many issues are accumulating, and we want to move beyond them to a state of tranquility. To help you to let go and relax into Creation, thus raising your vibration, you can try the following quick visualization exercise. Please note that in 'rising above' everything, I'm not implying that you are 'above' or better than anyone else. This is a method for moving beyond an accumulation of stressors or unhelpful perceptions.

1. Take about five minutes to relax. As you do so, focus on the mantra, 'My highest joy is in every moment.'

2. Next, visualize yourself outside, sitting on a soft carpet on the ground. It's a magic carpet, of course.

3. Observe the world around you, with its trivialities, stress, commotion, or anything you perceive as excessively challenging.

4. Notice the sounds.

5. Slowly, allow the magic carpet to rise with love above everything. As it does so, perceive less and less of the hullabaloo, comings and goings, activity, and the intensity of your desires and aims. All the noise from below begins to fade as you rise and enter the peaceful, tranquil space above.

6. Come to a stop. In silence, observe the colors, movement, and general shape of what's going on in the world below. You are above and away from it now, beyond its influence, having transcended everything.

7. Relax more, and settle down on the carpet. Feel the warmth of the sunshine and freshness of the gentle breeze.

8. Meditate here for as long as you wish, nonjudgmentally, not minding the world below. You've transcended everything while still remaining entirely present within the world.

9. End the meditation when you're ready and continue on afresh.

Your True Self, Purpose, and a Heart-Led Life

Are your actions aligned with your inner compass? It guides you in the direction your heart is pulling you toward, yet sometimes doubt creeps in: 'I can't make a living out of it.' 'I won't make a difference.' 'I don't have anything unique to offer.' These types of statements put a halt to your dreams before they've even had a chance to manifest.

Finding Your Purpose

During awakening and beyond, because our priorities change so much, our hopes and dreams naturally change. Some don't think about their purpose too much. Others feel they are living it just by being here, maybe enjoying spending time with loved ones, watching their kids grow up, or flowing with everyday experiences. There are those, however, who do seek a definite purpose but can't figure out what it is. Must you have a purpose? Certainly not, but for some it means everything.

In a way, for those who seek it, a purpose proves to them that they are alive. If you don't make your mark on the world, co-creating nothing, does it mean you are nothing? Of course not. How can you be nothing when you are an incarnation of universal consciousness? You are always something unique and wonderful, and you can start from there. Your consciousness, by its very nature, searches for experience, expansion, and growth, and meaningful purpose is a way to accommodate this. Sometimes, though, our ego only wants purpose to try to become something more. True purpose is more about experience, contribution, and creativity than it is about the superficial desires of the ego, so it's worth being mindful of that.

Some of the most fulfilled people I've met don't chase after enormous wealth; they become of service to others or the world in some way. So, first ask yourself: 'Am I searching for purpose in the right places? Am I driven by the wants, needs and aspirations that were given to me by others or society, or can I follow my heart?'

Your Heart Can Lead You to Your Calling

Your heart gives off powerful spiritual energy. We cannot measure this prana energy, the life-force of Creation that runs through us all, yet we can sense it and feel it. Your heart chakra is the energy center of love and understanding, your emotional guide, and it will help you find what you love to do, the endeavor that inspires your joy. Your soul also knows your purpose, so allow this wisdom to rise through your subconscious mind and intuitively pull you in the best direction. Allow your heart and soul to guide you in finding your true self and calling.

You don't know what you don't yet know. So if you still can't find your purpose, try hunting for one that ignites your passions. You can research professions, pastimes, and skills or observe what others are doing. Then, using your heart center and intuition, as you're considering ideas, observe which ones fill you with excitement. You might even gain inspiration for a totally unique idea. But what if you don't know where to start? Start with the things you love. Or think back to when you were a child. What did you love to do? Did you observe anyone else performing tasks that intrigued you?

Did you see something on TV or in a movie that made you go 'Wow!'? Even if it seems silly or trivial, use it to start your search. There might be a meaningful purpose in it, or it may lead you to something where you can make a real difference. When we feel excited, our heart center is activating, showing us the way.

It's worth remembering that your purpose may simply be to experience an earthly life, to raise the vibration through imparting your loving energies to others around you, or to have an enlightening experience. Just by being on your spiritual journey, you may walk past others and psychically affect them, triggering some sort of awakening in them.

When you find your heart-led purpose, consider pursuing it in your spare time if you work in a different field. You don't have to create a business out of it, and you may not wish to. But once you find your passion, others will likely be passionate about it too. Even if other people are providing the same product or service, it doesn't mean your unique offering won't also be in demand. Lastly, remember that in trying, failing, and trying again, we learn. Trial and error is part of learning. I followed my heart and intuitively found my purpose and then stuck to it. There were many ups and downs, a hundred hurdles to jump, but I never gave up. Now I've inspired millions of people all over the world, so my perseverance, for me, was worth it.

In sending out your intention to be the best co-creator you can be, the universe can't help but mirror this in your reality. You may well find that your purpose or ultimate fulfillment finds you at just the right time anyway; the universe is merely waiting until you are ready.

Imagination plays a key role in anything we create in reality. We can incorporate imaginative vision into our daily contemplation, not getting hopelessly lost in it, but playfully enjoying it.

> *Every child is an artist until he's told he's not an artist.*
>
> JOHN LENNON (ATTRIBUTED)

Everything that any human ever created started with an idea or vision, and without that, there would be no marvelous architecture, ethical organizations, art, poetry, writing, or anything else. Consider empathizing with the child you once were and recall some of the imaginative ideas you used to have. Someone may have told you to quit being a dreamer or to get your head out of the clouds, but now it's time to permit yourself to go there. As you relax into Creation and go with the flow, allow yourself to imagine even the impossible. Our preconceptions about many things being impossible only limit the universe in creating. Your imagination paints a picture for Creation to create. Ask yourself: 'What gifts am I bringing into the world?' We all have unique gifts to give, and in a moment of realization, we know what they are.

🦋 EXERCISE: CONNECTING WITH 🦋 YOUR INNER CHILD

To help you to discover your purpose you can rediscover your inner child's natural heart-led compass. Children often imagine things that adults have become conditioned to perceive as impossible. It's time to imagine as your younger self would. You can also perform a little healing at the same time.

1. Relax for 15 minutes while listening to meditation music.

2. Then imagine your favorite place when you were a child. Take your time and allow the scene to form within your inner vision.

3. Be as you are today, looking through your own eyes, present with your younger self. Be with them.

4. Either within your mind or out loud, tell them you love them, and ask if there is anything they'd like to talk about.

5. Provide reassurance, guidance, or advice as you feel appropriate.

6. Ask them if there was something in the whole world they'd love to do, what it would be.

7. Ask them what they would like to do or be when they grow up.

8. Thank them very much, provide a few more words of wisdom, and tell them you love them once more.

9. Allow the scene to fade and open your eyes when you're ready.

10. See if you can begin to reflect the dreams of your inner child in your life today.

Finding Your True Self Among Your Thoughts

Incessant thoughts put a dampener on daily well-being. In becoming your true self, it's vital to realize that you are not your ever-whirring thoughts. If you continually go over and over the contents of your mind, you're not truly experiencing the world. Have you ever had a day or an evening out and been so preoccupied with worries that you haven't been present to enjoy it? You're not creating meaningful new memories in that case. After all, you're missing everything that's going on around you, because you're in your head all the time. You're physically present, yes, but mentally somewhere else, either going over the past or worrying and planning for something in the future that might or might not happen. Can you find your true self among your thoughts? Who *are* you among them all?

We often make the mistake of thinking that our thoughts *are* us, when in actuality, they are fully immersive mini-stories happening within our minds. But if the thoughts are not us, and they are just happening to us, who is observing the thoughts?

> Stay present, and continue to be the observer
> of what is happening inside you. Become aware
> not only of the emotional pain but also of 'the
> one who observes,' the silent watcher.
>
> ECKHART TOLLE

Wow, so who is the silent watcher? Is it you? Perhaps it is the real you. When you become the observer of thoughts and emotions, you also become a pure point of awareness. In this state, there is only tranquility. The thoughts are over there, and you are over here, yet you can watch them without being controlled by them. In getting swept up in the stories of the mind, you miss out on life; but in observing and stepping outside of them, you see them for what they are, perhaps relentless habitual thinking, or sadness, or anxieties that require loving healing. In becoming only awareness, you release the pressure of the past and future, and exist only in an infinite present moment. The simplicity, sincerity, and purity of the *now* become apparent. Then, free of all else, your vibration can be whatever you allow it to be, perhaps love, appreciation, gratitude, or just peaceful, mindful awareness.

I'll Be Happy Once I...

Do desires equal joy? Will you be happy when you fulfill your desires? Or will you enjoy a fleeting moment of happiness, then earnestly start chasing the next desire? Where, then, does happiness lie? Probably always in the future rather than in this very moment.

In releasing some attachment to those things we want or already have, we are saying that they do not dictate who we are and that contentment is something we foster inside of ourselves. We all go over to 'the other side' and return to spirit eventually, and we can't take any of our physical possessions with us. This realization allows us to release some of our attachment to all that we have while remaining grateful that we have it. Change is a constant, and we can work on accepting that. Love and our loved ones, however, are eternal.

The Loving Approach

In using love as our go-to solution, many things change. It may be the ultimate truth, and our challenge is to realize it collectively. It's possible to reach a state of beingness where you view the world and everything in it with love, and this is beneficial for all. It sounds like a tall order. How can you have love for those who perform dastardly deeds? It seems impossible. But if the universe is one being, then when we hurt others, we are harming ourselves. When we love others, we're loving ourselves. Oneness means that every other being is part of us. Therefore, in radiating your love to others, you're healing the whole, everyone, and everything. If there are enough of us emanating love, when felt and expressed universally and unconditionally, it could initiate an incredible shift, a leap in the ascension of our collective consciousness.

> *Unconditional love really exists in each of us. It is part of our deep inner being. It is not so much an active emotion as a state of being. It's not "I love you" for this or that reason, not "I love you if you love me." It's love for no reason, love without an object.*
>
> RAM DASS

The more people who achieve this type of love, the more we heal collectively, and in turn, there will be more people who can radiate their love. One day we might reach a critical mass where love is the prevalent vibration.

Our perspective of every crisis or challenge changes when we view it through the lens of love, and in turn, solutions present themselves. You can ask yourself: 'What is the most loving way to approach this?' Of course, maintain your boundaries, and stand up for what's right, but what is the most love-based solution? The best way to combat fear and hatred is to cancel them out with the opposite vibration. The best solution is one implemented with understanding, care, and compassion. The truth of our existence is love, and many are under illusions that lead them away from it, but you can lead them back through example.

Shining the Light of Love Inward Too

Then there's self-love. How can you share your high vibration with the world if you direct unpleasant emotions toward yourself? Many of us have poor self-perception because we have been subject to put-downs, rejections, overly high expectations, neglect, prejudice, or ridicule, but this must no longer dictate who we are. We are usually subject to unfavorable circumstances or programming from people who have suffered from an absence of love. In going back to our past, we put these things right, and release such influences, and in turn, take down, brick by brick, our barriers to self-love.

> *You have been criticizing yourself for years, and it hasn't worked. Try approving of yourself and see what happens.*
> LOUISE HAY

Before barriers were built around it, our natural state was self-love. Young children naturally feel great about themselves, but often, very early on, this innate loving feeling is extinguished by others or our circumstances. It's important to bring ourselves back to that natural state, and self-acceptance can help us to do so. Self-acceptance leads to self-love. If you begin to notice and contemplate all the aspects of yourself that you reject, and instead consider accepting them, you are performing the groundwork for self-love. Can you accept all the things you'd usually criticize yourself for, and love yourself just the way you are? You can work on those aspects as part of your self-development practice, but still accept first that they are part of you. No one can possibly be perfect, yet we are perfect in all our imperfections. Start there. As we heal our backstories and cultivate self-acceptance, self-love naturally follows. Begin to notice your positive traits instead of ignoring them; celebrate your little wins. Pat yourself on the back for meeting a challenge and congratulate yourself for handling it well. You are very deserving.

Likewise, self-compassion also fosters self-love. Many people are extremely hard on themselves, lacking the understanding, care, sympathy, and forgiveness for themselves that they'd naturally show to others. When we assess our actions, reactions, thoughts, and behaviors, most of us often evaluate ourselves unfairly. If this is something you do as well, try to foster self-compassion instead. You'll begin to see things for what they are, eliminating unreasonable expectations and disregard for yourself. Care for yourself as you'd wish to be cared for, because we take care of those we love.

Consciousness Ever Rising

As you move through awakening and beyond, you may have traveled full circle, yet you're returning a very different person.

It's like the difference between a captive bird and a free bird. The captive is kept in a cage in someone's living room, with no idea of what's outside. The TV is on, the conditions are restrictive and monotonous, and the owner says what goes. The free bird, however, is subject to nobody, it can explore where it likes, its mind free from influence, choosing its own destiny. Perhaps you are now more like the free bird. Congratulations! You can see the fantastic potential it has. Close your eyes for a moment and visualize new possibilities, do so with absolutely no restrictions, let go completely. Dare to imagine.

There will likely still be accelerated phases of realization for you as time goes on, waves of transformation as you awaken to further revelations. You are an ever-evolving being, so you might reevaluate the nine *p*'s from time to time and implement further changes. Have trust in the process as well as in your power as a sovereign being. No one has it all figured out, but you're on the road to greater understanding. If you take control of your own destiny, others cannot dictate it for you. Claim your energy back from sources that seek to harness it or that reduce your well-being. Your energy is yours to use to create.

Cast off any unbeneficial labels that were applied to you or that you placed upon yourself, for you are a unique expression of all that is. Then observe any fear leave your mind and body as you become infinity. You are individual, yet you are everything – soul consciousness expressing boundless possibilities as an awakened human being.

You are one of the pioneers exploring a new frontier. A few hundred years from now, they'll remember those who began to think this way, outside the physical box, those who opened their eyes to the spiritual nature of self and reality. So keep up the fantastic work. We are manifesting the future now with every change we make and every action we take.

As for our inner worlds, we're healing and passing on the benefits to new generations, eliminating their future suffering. Times are a-changing, and as a result, global awakening is happening. Love, understanding, and the realization of oneness illuminate all shadows as a heart-led existence becomes the new norm. You're a sign of humanity's evolution, a brave explorer who rose to the challenge of spiritual awakening and journeyed through it and beyond. Your higher self is infinitely proud.

~

References

1. Maslow, A. H. (1943), 'A Theory of Human Motivation', *Psychological Review*, 50(4), 370–396.

2. Open Sciences (2014), '*The Manifesto for a Post-Materialist Science*': Open Sciences: opensciences.org/about/manifesto-for-a-post-materialist-science [Accessed 16 December 2020].

3. Cambridge Dictionary (2020), '*Cognitive Dissonance*'; dictionary.cambridge.org/dictionary/english/cognitive-dissonance [Accessed 16 December 2020].

4. NHS (2020), '*Psychosis*', www.nhs.uk/conditions/psychosis/ [Accessed 23 June 2020].

5. HeartMath Institute (2015), '*Science of the Heart, Exploring the Role of the Heart in Human Performance: An Overview of Research Conducted by the HeartMath Institute*', www.heartmath.org/research/science-of-the-heart/ [Accessed 16 December 2020].

6. ibid.

7. Jung, C. G. (1951), cited Main, R. (1997), *Jung on Synchronicity and the Paranormal*, London: Routledge.

8. Oschman, J. L., et al. (2015), 'The effects of grounding (earthing) on inflammation, the immune response, wound healing,

and prevention and treatment of chronic inflammatory and autoimmune diseases'. *Journal of Inflammation Research*, 8: 83–96.

9. Dispenza, J. (2017), *Becoming Supernatural: How Common People Are Doing the Uncommon*, California: Hay House Inc.

10. Research Gate. (2016), 'Taking a Closer Look at the Neglected "Pineal Gland" for Optimal Mental Health', www.researchgate. net/publication/309284646_Taking_a_Closer_Look_at_the_ Neglected_Pineal_Gland_for_Optimal_Mental_Healthnter_ title [Accessed 16 December 2020]

11. Watts, A. (lectures compiled in 1972), *'Mind over Mind – Part 1'*, The Alan Watts Organization, www.alanwatts.org/1-5-1-mind-over-mind-pt-1/ [Accessed 16 December 2020].

12. Wikipedia. (2020), *'Retrocausality'*, en.wikipedia.org/wiki/ Retrocausality [Accessed 16 December 2020].

13. Brewer, J. A., et al. (2011), 'Meditation experience is associated with differences in default mode network activity and connectivity', *PNAS* 108(50): 20254–20259.

14. Roy, R., cited Medvedeva, S. and Anisimov, V. (2006), *Water: The Great Mystery*, [Film].

15. Korotkov, K.G., cited Medvedeva, S. and Anisimov, V. (2006), *Water: The Great Mystery*, [Film].

Selected Bibliography

Campbell, Joseph. (1990). *The Hero's Journey: Joseph Campbell on His Life and Work*. California: New World Library.

———. (1991). *A Joseph Campbell Companion: Reflections on the Art of Living. The Collected Works of Joseph Campbell*. California: Joseph Campbell Foundation (JCF.org).

Dass, Ram. (2010). *Be Love Now: The Path of the Heart*, London: Rider.

Dyer, Wayne. (2014). *I Can See Clearly Now*, London: Hay House UK.

Global Consciousness Project. 'Meaningful Correlations in Random Data', noosphere.princeton.edu [Accessed 16 December 2020].

Grof, Stanislav and Christina Grof. (1989). *Spiritual Emergency: When Personal Transformation Becomes a Crisis*. Los Angeles: Jeremy P. Tarcher, Inc.

Hancock, Graham. (2015). *The Divine Spark, Psychedelics, Consciousness and the Birth of Civilization*. London: Hay House UK.

Hay, Louise. (2011). *The Golden Louise L. Hay Collection*, London: Hay House UK.

Jung, C.G. (1916). Cited Adler, G., et al. (1973), *C.G. Jung Letters: Volume 1 1906–1950*. London and New York: Routledge.

Jung, Carl. (1968). *Collected Works of C.G. Jung, Volume 12: Psychology and Alchemy*, New Jersey: Princeton University Press.

Liberman, Jacob. (1991). *Light: Medicine of the Future. How We Can Use It to Heal Ourselves Now*, Vermont: Bear & Company.

McKenna, Terence. Cited: Brown, J. B. (2013). *The New Science of Psychedelics: At the Nexus of Culture, Consciousness, and Spirituality*. Vermont: Park Street Press.

McTaggart, Lynne. (2001). *The Field: The Quest for the Secret Force of the Universe*. New York: Harper Collins Publishers Inc.

Reed, Henry. (1988). *Awakening Your Psychic Powers: Open Your Inner Mind and Control Your Psychic Intuition Today*. New York: St Martin's Press.

Singer, Michael. (2007). *The Untethered Soul: The Journey Beyond Yourself*, California: New Harbinger Publication, Inc.

Stanford Encyclopedia of Philosophy. (2019). 'Retrocausality in Quantum Mechanics,' plato.stanford.edu/entries/qm-retrocausality/ [Accessed 16 December 2020]

Stevenson, Ian. (2001). *Children Who Remember Previous Lives: A Question of Reincarnation*. Jefferson: McFarland & Company, Inc., Publishers.

Targ, Russell. (2004). *Limitless Mind: A Guide to Remote Viewing and Transformation of Consciousness*, California: New World Library.

Tesla, Nikola. (1919). *My Inventions: The Autobiography of Nikola Tesla* (2011). Eastford, CT: Martino Fine Books.

Three Initiates. (1908). *The Kybalion: A Study of The Hermetic Philosophy of Ancient Egypt and Greece.* Chicago: The Yogi Publication Society.

Tolle, Eckhart. (1999). *The Power of Now: A Guide to Spiritual Enlightenment*, London: Hodder & Stoughton Ltd.

———. (2005). *A New Earth: Create A Better Life.* London: Penguin Books.

Vivekananda, S. (1896). *The Complete Works of Swami Vivekananda: Mayavati Memorial Edition, Volume II, (1958).* Calcutta: Advaita Ashrama.

Watts, Alan. 'Out of Your Mind 11: The World as Emptiness (Part 1)', Seminar Transcript: www.organism.earth/library/document/out-of-your-mind-11 [Accessed 16 December 2020].

Wilde, Stuart. (1983). *Whispering Winds of Change: Perceptions of a New World.* Sydney: Nacson & Sons, then London: Hay House.

Williamson, Marianne. (1992). *A Return to Love: Reflections on the Principles of a Course in Miracles.* London: Harper Collins Publishers.

ABOUT THE AUTHOR

Nicky Sutton is a meditation and spiritual guide and a hypnosis practitioner whose YouTube videos have been watched more than 12 million times. With her compassionate and down-to-earth approach and broad spectrum of knowledge, she inspires and guides people through the process of spiritual awakening toward infinite metaphysical and mind-expanding possibilities. Having found little support during her own spiritual awakening, Nicky now devotes herself to offering knowledge and resources to others undergoing the same transformation toward higher consciousness. As well as writing and video making, she also creates inspiring guided meditations and hypnosis to allow spiritual seekers to heal energetically, and to journey deep within to explore the multidimensional nature of their consciousness.

f nickysuttonawakening

◎ nickysuttonawakening

🐦 @Nicky_Sutton_

You Tube Spiritual Awakening and
Guided Meditations with Nicky Sutton

www.nickysutton.com

Hay House Podcasts
Bring Fresh, Free Inspiration Each Week!

Hay House proudly offers a selection of life-changing audio content via our most popular podcasts!

Hay House Meditations Podcast

Features your favorite Hay House authors guiding you through meditations designed to help you relax and rejuvenate. Take their words into your soul and cruise through the week!

Dr. Wayne W. Dyer Podcast

Discover the timeless wisdom of Dr. Wayne W. Dyer, world-renowned spiritual teacher and affectionately known as "the father of motivation." Each week brings some of the best selections from the 10-year span of Dr. Dyer's talk show on Hay House Radio.

Hay House Podcast

Enjoy a selection of insightful and inspiring lectures from Hay House Live events, listen to some of the best moments from previous Hay House Radio episodes, and tune in for exclusive interviews and behind-the-scenes audio segments featuring leading experts in the fields of alternative health, self-development, intuitive medicine, success, and more! Get motivated to live your best life possible by subscribing to the free Hay House Podcast.

Find Hay House podcasts on iTunes, or visit www.HayHouse.com/podcasts for more info.

HAY HOUSE
Online Video Courses

Your journey to a better life starts with figuring out which path is best for you. Hay House Online Courses provide guidance in mental and physical health, personal finance, telling your unique story, and so much more!

LEARN HOW TO:

- choose your words and actions wisely so you can tap into life's magic

- clear the energy in yourself and your environments for improved clarity, peace, and joy

- forgive, visualize, and trust in order to create a life of authenticity and abundance

- break free from the grip of narcissists and other energy vampires in your life

- sculpt your platform and your message so you get noticed by a publisher

- use the creative power of the quantum realm to create health and well-being

To find the guide for your journey,
visit www.HayHouseU.com.

HAY HOUSE
online learning

HAY HOUSE

Look within

Join the conversation about latest products,
events, exclusive offers and more.

 Hay House

 @HayHouseUK

 @hayhouseuk

 healyourlife.com

We'd love to hear from you!